C000132712

Trollaval up Glen Dibidil

THE ISLAND OF

RHUM

A GUIDE FOR WALKERS, CLIMBERS
& VISITORS

HAMISH M. BROWN

CICERONE PRESS
MILNTHORPE, CUMBRIA

© Hamish M. Brown 1972, 1988
Reprinted 1978, 1980

Revised Edition 1988
Reprinted 1995

ISBN 1 85284 002 1

Other titles by Hamish Brown:

Hamish's Mountain Walk. (The Scottish Munros) *Gollancz/Granada.*
Hamish's Groat's End Walk. (English, Welsh, Irish Munros) *Gollancz/*
Granada.
The Great Walking Adventure. *Oxford Illustrated Press.*
Travels. (Articles from *The Scotsman*).
Time Gentlemen. (Collected Poems) *Aberdeen University Press.*
(Edited) Speak to the Hills and Poems of the Scottish Hills. *AUP.*
Five Bird Stories. *(Pettycur Publishing).*
Hamish Brown's Scotland. *Aberdeen University Press.*

Foreword and Acknowledgements

This guide departs from most climbing guides by giving information on a range of topics. Rhum, being an important National Nature Reserve is different (and finer) than most areas where we perform our rock antics and as such should appeal to a greater range of visitors.

Without the help of the Nature Conservancy Council this guide would not have been possible and the following I would like to thank personally: the present Director, Scotland, Dr John Francis, Dr J. Morton Boyd, his predecessor, whose warm preface is reprinted here, Martin Ball, John Love, Mr Peter Wormell, the island's first Chief Warden and Mr J. Laughton Johnston, the Chief Warden 1986, as well as the many staff members and researchers who gave of their time.

All these helped in many ways to ensure Part I is as accurate as possible. Part II owes a great deal to Anne Littlejohn of the Ladies Scottish Climbing Club who put together a card index of climbs and to the Scottish Mountaineering Club Journal editor who has recorded new routes since. The late Ian Clough also contributed notes and the late Gavin Maxwell allowed me to quote a passage from his book "Harpoon at a Venture". Some earlier writings on Rhum climbing are noted in the bibliography. Various people have helped with the illustrations and my thanks to them. Photographs not acknowledged are my own. The drawings of shearwaters and sea eagles are the work of Ian Strachan – many thanks – and likewise to Sheila Gallimore for her typing work over many months.

Part I has largely been re-written for a number of interesting developments and studies have occurred since 1972 – notably the reintroduction of the sea eagle – and practical information is all too apt to change. (The old *Loch Arkaig* sank for instance!). The Ordnance Survey 1:50,000 map sheet 39 is the most readily available useful map and should be used in conjunction with this guide.

Hamish M. Brown
Kinghorn 1987

+ + + Forest Boundary

Area for climbing by authorised parties

KILMORY

Samhnan Moir

DEER AREA

Camas Pliasgaig

Glen Shellesder

Kilmory Glen

Mullach Mor

NORTH SIDE

GUIRDIL

Rubha na Roinne

Fionchra

Kinloch Glen

A' Bhrideanach

Bloodstone Hill

Minishal

B a Bhraig Bhig

Stable Flats

Waterfall

KINLOCH

LOCH SCRESORT

Castle Pier

Port n Carane

Orval

Long Loch

Corrie Dubh

SOUTH SIDE

Schooner Point

Ard Nev

Wreck Bay

Lag Sleitir

BARKEVAL, 1924

Bealach Barkeval

HALLIVAL

2365

Bagh' h-Uam

Glen Duian

L Monica

B an Oir

Glen Harris

Mausoleum

HARRIS

TROLLAVAL ▲ 2300

B an Fhuarain

ASKIVAL 2659

Welshma Rock

L Fiachinis

AINSHVAL ▲ 2552

Glen Dibidil

Sgurr nan Geibhrean

Beinn nan Stac

Sgor an t-Snide.

RUINSIVAL, 1607

SGURR NAN GILLEAN, 2503

Stac nam Faoileann.

Fist and Finger Stack.

DIBIDIL

0   Approx. scale in Miles   1

PAPADIL

Loch Papadil

Papadil Pinnacin.

Sron na h-Iolaire

Rubha nam Meirleach

SKYE

CANNA

RHUM

●Mallaig

EIGG

MUCK

6

Preface to the Original Edition

The track to Bloodstone Hill runs over the Pass between Fionchra and Orval. The going is soft, the air is light and the sunshine flecks the landscape. As you go, you become tucked away among grassy hills in company with red deer, pipits and constellations of small brilliant wild flowers. Dark green fritilleries flutter in sun-trap gullies and streams gush noisily, pure and clear. The final reward is a view from the top of the Bloodstone; there suddenly you are on a lofty balcony; below is Canna and Sanday and a panorama of mountains, blue islands and distant peaks. You are alone with Rhum and you know perhaps for the first time, its massive strength of character, and you are thrilled by the seductive charm of wild, sequested country.

Rhum is an island with a difference! Following the emigration of the Native population and a century of private ownership, during which visitors were discouraged, the island became known as "forbidden". The sense of the macabre is often heightened by its bare, hard outline, dark bemisted coolins and its rather grand but oddly aloof mansion house. That it should have become a nature reserve – even one of the grandest in Britain – was almost certain to be interpreted as a further deepening of its shuttered gloom rather than a new welcoming and smiling island. Some who live in the past no doubt see it yet as that, but they have never savoured the welcome of the Chief Warden and his staff with their families of laughing children or the splendid experience which awaits the day tripper, the camper, the senior schoolboy (or girl) and student on residential projects and the climber. Of course, there are some "dos" and "don'ts" as there are for all nature reserves but these are the minimum required to provide safeguard for wildlife and the work of the scientist. Of the thousands who visit the island over the years, few complain of unreasonable restriction to their freedom!

Geologist, naturalist, historian and climber alike, have Rhum as a happy hunting ground. Hamish Brown, the ardent far-travelled mountaineer and exuberant writer has done a service to all, including the Nature Conservancy who own the island, by providing this guide. Rhum is not a land set aside entirely for the expert or specialist but it does have something quite exclusive to offer those who have an eye for detail. There is probably no other island of comparable size in the world which is so well documented in its flora, fauna, rocks and ruins and so well staffed by knowledgable men who know and love the island. There is access to all the hills depending on the scientific work in progress, but the number of people on the range at any one time is necessarily smaller than on most mainland peaks. Accredited mountaineers find the ridge paths green, often unmarked and the rock faces quiet. Though visitors are asked not to collect, there are few rocks, plants or animals the identity of which is not known to the staff who, given a description, can usually provide a name rather than a specimen to take away. Wild, grand and beautiful country like Rhum will only remain so if it is properly cared for. The serenity of wilderness is apt to be shattered by too many people; for the small numbers who go to Rhum there must be a never-to-be-forgotten experience – a fine, strong liqueur taken in small measure – something cherished and never abused.

Hamish Brown has provided a comprehensive summary of scientific and cultural interests, a description of the short but challenging climbs and a great deal of up-to-date information about access and facilities as well. For what more could one ask about a so-called forbidden isle!

J. Morton Boyd.
28-1-72.

Contents

Sgur Mhor, view from Camasnáhátha, Inverness-shire
Photo by John Leng & Co. Ltd.

Part One: General

INTRODUCTION

The Inner Hebridean Island of Rhum is still an island of mystery to many people, perhaps because the memory still lingers of former landed gentry who discouraged visitors by every means possible. It is an island which delightfully combines interest for both climber and naturalist. The Nature Conservancy Council bought the Island in 1957 and now manage it as a National Nature Reserve. It became a Biosphere Reserve in 1977 under the Man & the Biosphere (UNESCO) programme. They have evolved a happy system to accommodate the demands of both their own important work and those of visitors. As Rhum possesses interesting peaks, climbers who enjoy leaving the beaten track have always headed for them.

Those who have penetrated its hidden cliffs and corries and walked its high ridges often return with almost a sense of pilgrimage accomplished. It has been compared to a golfer having visited St. Andrews for a round on the Old Course. Certainly when one is pub gossiping and discovers someone else who has been to Rhum, then much swopping of experiences will follow. Few people visit Rhum once only. Each has his own story. Take a passage from *Harpoon at a Venture* by Gavin Maxwell.

"Rhum is a strange place, eerie and haunted if ever a Hebridean island was. It is all mountain – hills as dark and savage as the Cuillins themselves, and falling for the most part steeply to the sea. The hills even carry the name, the Cuillin of Rhum, but they seem to have a different soul, something older and more brooding. Their names are mainly Norse, given them long ago by the raiding longships . . . if there is a place where I could believe every Gaelic folk-tale and wild superstition it is in their shadow. I know a man who found himself in a high corrie of Askival with a dead stag after dusk. His coat was clutched and he felt himself being dragged uphill while from right below his feet a voice seemed as if in an extremity of fear".

It is the imaginative writer rather than the scientist coming out in that passage, for the charm of Rhum is its combination of interest in mountain form, climbing potential, a varied and fascinating wildlife, and serious research. Anyone interested in one aspect only will miss half the enjoyment. Satisfaction rarely lies in extremes; in Rhum we have the happy medium to satisfy everyone.

NAMES

The spelling of Rhum or Rum is open to debate but as the Nature Conservancy Council owners choose to use RHUM, linguists who tend to favour RUM, will have to thole it. Anyway, who wants to write a post card home reporting he'd been on Rum for a week? It was perhaps for such delicate reasons that the Sassenach Victorians in fact added the "h" to Rum. The Ordnance Survey is happy with RHUM on its maps.

The name may be pre-Celtic though the thought that it embodies the root of Greek word *rhombos* in allusion to its shape rather stretches credibility. It would need a bird's eye view (or a modern map) to show its dumpy-diamond shape. In the *Description of the Western Isles of Scotland* (1549) Sir Donald Monro gave the name as *Ronin*. The original would appear to be the Norse *Röm öe* meaning wide, spacious island; shortening to Ruma, Rum, pronounced more correctly ROOM, as Gaelic has no "Rh-" prefix.

The VAL (hill) and DIL (vale) endings to names are also Norwegian. There is no evidence of Viking settlement; these were landmarks of use to passing ships.

SITUATION

This Inverness-shire island on the 57th parallel covers 26,400 acres, is about 8 miles from north to south and about the same from east to west. Landing on Rhum is like stepping onto a mountain slope; as though some western range had been lopped off and floated out the 15 miles from the mainland. The only real indentation and safe harbour in the 28 miles of coastline is Loch Scresort on the east; the rest is cliff or boulder bays except for Bagh na h-Uamha and a few northern strands whose golden sands can clearly be seen from the Cuillin of Skye, ten miles to the north. The view from Skye's Coir' a Ghrunnda over Soay to Rhum is one of Scotland's finest. From the mainland, weather and lighting can make the island appear to come nearer or recede to an unusual degree. In combination with Eigg, four miles to the south east, the view from the mainland of Morar also gives that balanced beauty of sky, peak and sea that is Scotland's western glory.

At Schooner Point and Wreck Bay the sea cliffs reach nearly 1,000 ft. and at Dibidil great clefts run into the land; everywhere there are stacks and pinnacles – and always the noise of the sea.

Kinloch and Loch Scresort form a secretive, gentle touch of softness and civilisation, perhaps only the width of a belt of trees, but

12

Rhum from Eigg

creating a world of its own, which the day visitor admires and the climber relishes after the bleak hinterland.

Two miles to the west lie Canna and Sanday while south beyond Eigg is Muck and about nine miles to the west lies the reef of Oigh-Sgeir with its lonely lighthouse. All these collectively, bear the title "The Parish of the Small Isles".

THE NATURE CONSERVANCY

Rhum had been a sporting estate for over a century when the Nature Conservancy Council bought the island in 1957 to establish the third largest National Nature Reserve in Britain and use it as an "outdoor laboratory". Peter Wormell came from jungly African forest surveys to become the first Chief Warden. He married a local lass and only moved on in 1974. He added over fifty species of moths and butterflies to the Rhum list and built up a valuable collection. A score of new plants were discovered by him. Bivouacs on the hills were accepted as part of his Shearwaters research. A busy life, yet with the calm of the researcher – needed at times, as when seven years of tree planting go up in flames. The first Senior Warden was George McNaughton (till 1974), whose family had been on Rhum for over

13

half a century.

There are 7 families whose menfolk work full time for the Nature Conservancy as estate staff. Their duties encompass a great range of skills: stalking, handling ponies and cattle, general farm work, forest nursery work and tree planting, fencing, draining, roadwork, refuse disposal, plumbing, electrical and mechanical maintenance and butchering. To ensure a continuity of schooling married staff with young families are employed on Rhum – which can lead to some low average-age statistics for the island!

The Royal Charter setting up the Nature Conservancy in 1949 states the functions thus: To provide scientific advice on the conservation and control of the natural flora and fauna of Great Britain; to establish, maintain and manage nature reserves in Great Britain, including the maintenance of physical features of scientific interest; and to organise and develop the research and scientific services related thereto.

ACCESS

The Nature Conservancy Council controls access to the island and authorisation should be obtained by visitors intending to stay there. Safety needs and Conservancy work make it essential that only recognised climbing clubs or similar groups (minimum of four persons), all completely self-contained, be permitted to camp and climb in the designated area. Club Group secretaries or visiting scientists or naturalists should contact the Chief Warden, Rhum NNR, the White House, Isle of Rhum, by Mallaig, Scotland (0687-2026) about their rough plans and dates. These may have to be adjusted to fit in with others' bookings at peak periods but the Nature Conservancy Council do their best to fit everyone in. Relevant, up-to-date information sheets are available from the Chief Warden and these are useful as some of the details below may alter from year to year.

To exclude Man entirely from the island could only create an ecologically false situation; Man, for better or – so often – for worse, is a factor in natural development. Rhum demonstrates how he need not be a destructive element.

The Nature Conservancy Council can accept no rescue liability or calls on its staff and parties are asked to comply with any local arrangements or restrictions. Sometimes the island may be "closed" for scientific work. If in doubt consult the Chief Warden.

Rhum is normally reached from Mallaig, the nearest port on the mainland. As Mallaig is the terminus of the West Highland Railway it is possible to travel up to Mallaig and cross to Rhum remarkably easily. Motor cars may be left for a small fee at the friendly West Highland Hotel (0687-2210). The nearest Youth Hostel is Garramore, twelve miles from Mallaig (April-September). There are many Bed and Breakfast facilities in Mallaig, plenty of shops and petrol is available.

The main sailings are operated by Caledonian MacBrayne Ltd., The Ferry Terminal, Gourock (0475-33755). There is a local office on Mallaig pier (0687-2403). This gives a regular service on Monday, Wednesday, Thursday and Saturday by the steamer *Lochmor*. Passengers transfer to and from the steamer in Loch Scresort by the Conservancy ferryboat *Rhouma*. It leaves the Jetty ahead of *Lochmor's* time so be early when leaving the island.

(Rhouma is one of the older spellings of the island and was used, formerly for Sir George Bullough's steam yacht. It was also the name of an aged pony which was destroyed an hour or two before the new ferryboat sailed into Loch Scresort!)

On Tuesdays and Thursdays, (Easter to September) the *Shearwater* sails to Rhum from Arisaig. Contact Murdo Grant, Arisaig Marine Ltd, Arisaig Harbour (06875-224/678). Outwith this period *Shearwater* can be chartered; also *The Western Isles*, Bruce Watt Cruises, Mallaig Pier (0687-2233). It is sometimes possible to hire a boat from Elgol or Glenbrittle in Skye and in the summer there are sometimes excursion sailings anyway. The Nature Conservancy Council boat is not normally available for public use apart from meeting scheduled steamers. Check current timetables as these may alter with little warning. Loch Scresort is the only safe anchorage and landings elsewhere are discouraged except in very special circumstances.

The Nature Conservancy Council staff, though busy men engaged in various duties, are glad to advise and help and the good ladies of the island sometimes provide teas with home baking in the community hall when larger excursions are visiting for the day. Two Nature Trails have been laid out: one along the south side of Loch Scresort, the other up Kinloch Glen (trail guides available at Kinloch). Day visitors are asked not to go beyond this area; in fact they seldom have either time or footwear to make this desirable. The North Side is reserved for research work and is only "open" on Sunday but the whole southern half is available for authorised climbing parties.

There are toilet facilities by the pier and picnic places along the

Dibidil Bothy with Askival behind

shore for day visitors. The Castle is open for public tours. Dogs should not be brought ashore.

ACCOMMODATION

There is a range of accommodation – from castle opulence to midgy camping: 2 open bothies, NCC bunk houses (for official or voluntary work parties), Bed and Breakfast, and hostel or hotel quarters in Kinloch Castle. Camping is the normal procedure and all foods, fuels and other needs should be brought. In emergencies orders could be phoned from the box at the Post Office to Mallaig shops who may send orders by boat. The Post Office (0687-2032) now sells sweets, cake, biscuits, lemonade, beer, peanuts and various souvenirs.

The Nature Conservancy Council and the Mountain Bothies Association (through a generous grant by the late E. W. Hodge) with their work parties restored a bothy at strategic Dibidil, which is open for free use by climbers. Mr Hodge, in the bad old days, was sent to Coventry by the Estate on owner's orders for refusing to leave the Island when told – and retaliated by forcing the Post Office to sell him their entire stock of stamps, which of course they had to do.

Dibidil's only drawback is a complete lack of driftwood as there is no open shore. Guirdill is another restored bothy on the north coast under Bloodstone Hill. These may be used (useful bases) by visitors. The small lodge at Harris has been renovated but it is not available for climbers, Papadil was allowed to go to ruin as it was really of no use as a base. Campers use the shore of Loch Scresort (there is a small charge) and camping elsewhere is not allowed. Camping may be made interesting by cuckoos, midges and rain – in any combination! Water and toilet facilities are on site.

LITTER

There is no public disposal service and visitors are asked to assist the estate staff by burning litter where possible and using the camp site bins. Fires are only permitted on the site.

KINLOCH CASTLE

Kinloch Castle (an Edwardian mansion) is open during the summer season. Some of the front rooms provide self-service and self-catering accommodation for visitors. The back rooms provide self-service and self-catering accommodation for courses, staff, research workers and other visitors. The Castle is also open to the public at certain times, when the caretakers provide a conducted tour. Interested parties should make enquiries on arrival. (See HISTORY for its story.)

INTERNAL TRAVEL

Only shank's pony can be relied on. Soft-hearted staff in their Land Rovers may give the odd lift to rucksacks or climbers but this should not be expected. There is an elementary unsurfaced road system running from Kinloch for seven miles, maximum height at Lag Sleitir, 850 ft., to flowery Harris on the west coast, with a branch going north to Kilmory from the head of Kinloch Glen at 300 ft.

An important footpath follows up Coire Dubh by the Allt Slugan to a dam beyond a small gorge whence it is easy to pick a route up to the Bealach Barkeval at about 1,550 ft. (Do not touch the rain gauge in Coire Dubh). From the col easy access can be had for Hallival and Barkeval or down into the Atlantic Corrie and Glen Harris – no path though. See the introduction to Part Two for other walking information.

To gain the Coire Dubh path cross the stile from the west side of

Kinloch Castle; with some of the Rhum ponies

the bridge over the Rockery Burn (signposted) and follow the burn up through the field and through a small gate, then on to pass the generator house and reach the open hillside by another gate in a wall.

The other important path for climbers begins about 50 yards east of the Gates on the "back" road. It is probably most easily found by walking along from the jetty in the Post Office direction. Just beside the first house a small burn runs down. Go up it to the "back" road and the hill path continues on beyond in the same direction. It is clearly signposted. The six mile track wends up southwards for 600 ft and contours with undulations to Dibidil. Maximum height, above Welshman's Rock, is about 750 ft. (This name came from Welsh masons who cut a ledge across the cliff in the last century to enable sheep to escape its dangers). The path is splendidly set above the sea. Even in severe storms the various burns are all – amusingly – passable. A less distinct path from Dibidil, rising to 550 ft., reaches Papadil two and a half miles further on but beyond that there is no track to Harris and cliffs force the walker to about the 700 ft. contour. These paths are worth noting as the terrain seldom gives easy going. It is fairly easy also to ascend Glen Dibidil to the Bealach an Oir (the

The approach to the Slugan
Path for Bealach Barkeval

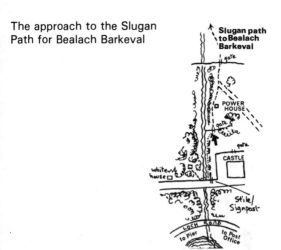

Pass of Gold, 1,550 ft.) for Glen Harris, or the Bealach an Fhuarain
(1,730 ft.) for the Fiachanis Corrie and Harris. For Harris – Ruinsival
approach see notes on that crag, page 00.

Paths on the North side. 1. To Glen Shellesder, as on map 2.
Across the Stable Flats, over the Bealach a' Bhraigh Bhig to
Bloodstone Hill. The Chief Warden can always be consulted for
planned walks here and (for all areas), the board outside his house
indicates day-by-day areas which may be under temporary restriction.

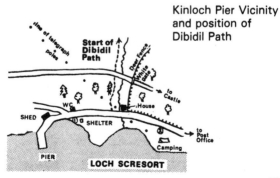

Kinloch Pier Vicinity
and position of
Dibidil Path

RAINFALL

Some statistics from 1958-1981 reveal April and May as the driest, October and November as the wettest months. On 16.1.81 Kinloch received a record 91.3mm. The averages for the period are revealing: Kinloch 2441mm, Kilmory 1853mm, Harris 1452mm.

NATURE TRAILS

South Side Nature Trail

About three miles out and back along the south shore of Loch Scresort. Cairn No. 1 is beside the slipway where trail leaflets are available from the box. The ground is frequently boggy or rough. Allow 2 hours. A return from Point 7 will take about 1 hour. The route follows through the planted trees, past the school house and over the South Wood. Insect-eating plants abound. A solitary grave and several old "black houses" point to relatively recent settlement, and rough moorland beyond leads to Port na Caranean, where the ruins of the Skye folk (evicted in the 1840's) are now the home of nesting eider and noisy gulls. Seals and otters may be seen and snipe heard "drumming" in the gloaming.

Kinloch Glen Nature Trail

Four miles out and back: along to the head of Loch Scresort and up Kinloch Glen. A good Land Rover track makes it an easy walk. Trail leaflets are available at the start by the pier. The route goes along the shore road with the plantation woods and Nature Conservancy Council houses on the left, the loch on the right. A Cotoneaster-covered wall hides the Castle policies. Behind the farm is the community hall. The turning up into Kinloch Glen is a pleasant spot.

A glance here once showed a visitor a Gold Crest, a Golden Eagle and a Corncrake, just like that! There are many pink and white foxgloves inside the wood. The Rhum ponies may be encountered on this walk and across the river lies the only farmland and the more recent tree planting on the North Side. The last mile is more featureless country and Point 8 is often a good point of return – above it to the south is the Bealach Mhic Neill Waterfall, probably the finest on the island, and, beside the road, a rocking stone (an erratic boulder).

THE FARM

Hay is grown on about eleven acres to provide winter feed for the ponies (used for stalking) and the Highland Cattle herd. The Rhum

Rhum ponies - a mare and foal at Kinloch

ponies are an old breed, perhaps introduced by the Vikings. (They are very like present day Icelandic ponies.) One unconfirmed story goes that the beginnings were due to the wreck of a ship from the Spanish Armada. They are variously coloured and are partly used as pack beasts, but most spend the winters free on the hill. They were known to Dr Johnson in 1771 when he reported, "the horses are very small but of a breed eminent for beauty". They never exceed 14 hands. Some are of dun colouring with an eel-streak along the back

Cattle on the shore at Guirdil - a view out of the bothy door

and conservation of this Western Isles breed is in progress. Numbers are kept at about twenty. Between the Second World War and 1957 there was a herd of about 50 beef cattle and up to 1,200 breeding ewes and gimmers. There are no sheep now – which allows better grass growth. On cliffs and glens of the south and west coast there are also Wild Goats.

In 1971 a small herd of Highland Cattle was introduced and they are now based on Harris Bay. Their transportation gave some excitement as the beasts objected to being herded on to the Knoydart Estate's landing craft *Spanish John*, broke loose and turned the streets of Mallaig into something akin to Pamplona in the bull festival. It would be advisable to treat them with a certain respect. They play an important role in keeping the vegetation cover healthy round Harris.

WILD ANIMALS

The Goats numbered 180 in 1985, are mainly dark, shaggy beasts, some with fine sweeping horns. They are not difficult to find round the coastal cliffs or in the mountains, particularly in the west. Their numbers are controlled largely by the weather and they are no longer culled. They are the decendants of domestic stock.

Rhum has no Roe deer, Voles, House mice, Hares, Rabbits, Moles, Squirrels, Foxes, Hedgehogs, Wild cats or Pine martens. There are Otters and both Grey and Common seals.

The island has its own Long-tailed field mouse however:

The wild goats of Rhum - on the shore at Dibidil

Apodemus sylvaticus hamiltoni, (recorded even on the summit of Hallival), Pygmy shrew, Pipistrelle bat and Brown rat (mainly on shore but a domestic nuisance in autumn/winter).

Reptiles and amphibians are represented solely by the Common lizard and Palmate newt; Frogs, Toads, Slow worms and Snakes are all absent.

Brown and Sea trout are common, so is the Common eel and Three-spined sticklebacks are found in Papadil Loch. Salmon occasionally are found at the mouth of the Kinloch River.

With the first Chief Warden an expert on *Lepidoptera* we can say little; perhaps just to mention Belted Beauty *(Nyssia zonaria)* and the flourishing Transparent Burnet *(Zygaena purpuralis)* – or retell of his leaving a bath to chase a Vestal moth which had probably strayed from France or Spain. Grayling, Large and Small Heath are the commonest butterflies; Fox, Drinker, Northern Eggar and Emperor the commonest moths.

A total of 2158 species of insect have been recorded. A brief breakdown indicates: Mayflies 15, Dragonflies 10, Stoneflies 12, Grasshoppers 4, Bugs 259, Alderflies/Lacewings 10, Butterflies/Moths 448, Caddisflies 43, Beetles 523, Ants/Bees/Wasps 235, Flies 550.

Fifty-one species of Spiders were recorded in a 1964 survey.

Visitors will be made aware of the presence of both biting Midges and Sheep ticks. The latter are prepared to wait years for a juicy human victim. The deer too suffer from parasites; the Nose bot fly (whose larvae lives in the nostrils of deer) looks in fact like a Bumble bee at first glance. The Dragonflies are very attractive, look out for the Blue Aeshna. A mountain-top Cixid bug is known only in Scotland, Snowdonia and Czechoslovakia.

The sea shore has perhaps been most neglected by visiting scientists. Whelks are sometimes collected commercially. The Gulf Stream has some effect for species found normally only further south have been recorded off the western coast of Scotland (eg Cornish sucker fish, usually associated with the Mediterranean and the Scilly Isles).

RED DEER

An island gives a fine contained environment for deer studies. Red deer are the only type found. Persecution wiped them out in the 18th century but since re-introduction to the island in 1845 numbers have grown to the present maintained level of about 1500. The Nature Conservancy Council are engaged in various studies and already results obtained are serving as a basis for conservation and management throughout the country. Deer are one of the main Highland exports and the years of study on Rhum have assisted the

Deer crossing the mouth of the Kinloch Burn

understanding of the species. There is a sheet available from the Chief Warden giving some details of this work and some books are listed in the bibliography. The annual deer cull is about one-sixth (a national figure derived from Rhum researches) and venison is exported from Rhum. Stalkers' courses are held each year.

In 1972 a unique long-term study commenced in the North Block (Kilmory), under Dr Tim Clutton-Brock and Fiona Guiness. The NCC agreed to stop their cull and the deer are left to live as "naturally" as possible. Every beast is known and studied throughout its life – a concentrated study only possible in a place like Rhum – and some interesting and unexpected results are already being noted. There are about 350 beasts in this area which is closed (except on Sundays) to minimise disturbance. (See bibliography.)

ORNITHOLOGY

Apart from seabirds, few birds enjoy any widespread distribution. Many owe their presence to the existence of the Loch Scresort woodlands, farmland and castle grounds. Several birds have been restored due to the new plantings while others, like the corncrake, have declined due to influences in other countries. Rhum is an island of great interest for the bird watcher.

The Nature Conservancy Council in 1984 listed 194 species of birds recorded on Rhum. However, as most visiting parties are likely to be on the island during the summer season the following abbreviated list may be useful. The office has reference copies of the full checklist and can give up-to-date information.

RED-THROATED DIVER
Breeds. Listen for their "loon" cries as they descend to Harris Bay or Loch Scresort to feed in the evening.

FULMAR
400 breeding pairs.

MANX SHEARWATER
Extensive mountain colonies (see note below).

GANNET
Seen offshore only.

CORMORANT
Occasional vagrant.

SHAG
Breeds round south shore.

GREYLAG GOOSE
Some breed.

HERON
Loch Scresort breeding occasionally.

MALLARD
A few.

EIDER
Common. Its "shocked-old-ladies" OH-OH cry familiar round Loch Scresort. Nests of "down" easily found (eg Port na Caranean).

RED-BREASTED MERGANSER
Increasing in numbers.

SHELDUCK
Occasional breeder, Kilmory.

GOLDEN EAGLE
3-4 pairs breed.

WHITE-TAILED EAGLE
Re-introduced (see below).

SPARROWHAWK
1 pair Kinloch.

PEREGRINE
1-2 breeding pairs usually.

MERLIN
1-3 breeding pairs, decreasing

KESTREL
1-2 breeding pairs usually.

RED GROUSE
Resident. Increasing slowly.

PTARMIGAN
Rare – probably from Skye.

CORNCRAKE
Now rare.

OYSTERCATCHER (Pied Piper)
Familiar sight and sound.

PEEWIT (Lapwing)

RINGED PLOVER
A few breed.

GOLDEN PLOVER
Regular breeder.

SNIPE
Breeds. "Drumming" caused by air rushing over extended feathers at base of tail can often be heard, especially at dusk.

WOODCOCK
Kinloch. "Roding" flight may be heard in gloaming.

CURLEW
Burbling cry distinctive; increasing.

COMMON SANDPIPER
Kinloch and Papadil sees this charming noisy summer visitor.

GREENSHANK
Passage only.

GREATER BLACK-BACKED GULL

LESSER BLACK-BACKED GULL

HERRING GULL

COMMON GULL

KITTIWAKE
About 1100 pairs. At Papadil Loch observed splashing on their backs!

ARCTIC TERN
Very few breed.

RAZORBILL
Colonies. 400 pairs.

GUILLEMOT
About 900 pairs.

BLACK GUILLEMOT
Mainly seen offshore.

PUFFIN
Few small colonies.

ROCK DOVE
Rocky shores.

WOODPIGEON
Increasing.

COLLARED DOVE
Now breeding.

CUCKOO
Omnipresent.

LONG-EARED OWL
Vagrant.

SHORT-EARED OWL
1-3 pairs breed.

SKYLARK
Scarce.

SWALLOW
Insect eating: to be encouraged!

DUNNOCK
Resident.

MEADOW PIPIT
Abundant.

ROCK PIPIT
Coastal.

PIED WAGTAIL
Kinloch and elsewhere.

GREY WAGTAIL
Irregular breeder.

WREN
Loud song for tiny bird.

DIPPER
On most rivers.

MISTLE THRUSH
Irregular breeder.

SONG THRUSH
Resident.

RING OUZEL (MOUNTAIN BLACKBIRD)
Nests in rocky places.

BLACKBIRD
Kinloch, common. Breaks whelks on shore, as if snails.

WHEATEAR
On rough slopes.

STONECHAT
Bright additions to rough scenery.

WHINCHAT
Breeds most years.

REDSTART
Irregular.

ROBIN
Many. Kinloch.

WHITETHROAT
Rare.

CHIFFCHAFF
Few breed most years.

WILLOW WARBLER
Common, Kinloch and now new plantings.

WOOD WARBLER
Kinloch area, occasionally.

GOLDCREST
Kinloch area.

SPOTTED FLYCATCHER
Kinloch/Papadil.

RAVEN
A few pairs of this real mountain bird.

HOODIE CROW
Breeds. Shoreline scavenger. "Anvils" behind Kinloch trees.

GREAT TIT
Usually only 1 pair.

BLUE TIT
Up to 10 pairs.

COAL TIT
Loch Scresort woods.

LONG-TAILED TIT
Irregular.

TREE-CREEPER
Few pairs, Kinloch.

STARLING
A few. Farm. Shore.

REDPOLL
Kinloch area, occasionally.

SISKIN
Kinloch area, occasionally.

TWITE
Kinloch area.

CHAFFINCH
Some very tame, Kinloch.

HOUSE SPARROW
Not in large numbers.

Manx Shearwater

This list does not include many passage migrants or winter visitors. Peter Wormell tells of one migrant extraordinary. He ringed a Blackbird at Kinloch one spring and later received information of its recapture in Denmark where it was given a second ring and released. This Blackbird, with two rings, was later again hopping about at Kinloch!

The *Manx Shearwater* is however the bird one associates most with Rhum. They may be seen skimming the waves out to sea as boats approach and in the evening rafts of many thousands gather, often between Rhum and Eigg. They nest, as nowhere else in Britain, in mountain-top burrows, which can be spotted afar by the green grass below them. Silence during the day time from the vast, invisible colony gives way to a frightful din at night when the birds swop incubation shifts. Trollaval, peak of the trolls, may owe its name to these inhabitants with their unworldly noise. In the Faroes too (cf the Gavin Maxwell quote) there are places where the word "troll" is associated with Shearwater colonies.

Eventually the one egg hatches. Before the chicks can fully fly the parents take off for destinations unknown (South Atlantic suspected) and the youngsters are left to tumble 1,500 ft. or more down to the sea unaided. There has been research on marked burrows and many birds have been ringed – the furthest recapture being Brazil. They will even travel to fish in the Bay of Biscay during the breeding season and recent evidence points to new breeding stations starting

White-tailed sea eagle

in Newfoundland. One ringed bird recovered was so marked 25 years ago. There are as many as 120,000 nesting pairs – the largest colony of this species. The Rhum Eagles have been seen circling by moonlight and from remains examined it seems their nocturnal flights are aimed at Shearwaters.

There is a wider variety of habitat on Rhum than in many similar places. The plantation of Kinloch trees give shelter to many birds. New plantations at Kilmory and Harris attract growing numbers of species as they develop. Persecuted species, like Merganser or Grouse are now increasing. But among those now extinct or gone are two Petrels, Gannet, introduced Game birds, Chough, and White-tailed Sea Eagle.

That last sentence was written in 1972, since when a new chapter has been written in the story of Scotland's White-tailed Sea Eagle (erne): *Haliaeetus albicilla*. In 1986 John Love wrote to me:

"It began in 1975, with the release of three young eagles from Norway. This has been repeated each year, sometimes with as many as ten being imported, until by 1985, a total of 82 had been released. Seven have since been found dead, one having collided with power lines, and two others being poisoned (a totally illegal practise and indeed, all birds of prey are strictly protected). However, the other eagles have adapted well to the wild, living on a diet of seabirds, fish and carrion.

"White-tailed Eagles take some five years to reach sexual

A dead shearwater on the Rhum peaks

maturity, and it is only recently that the Reintroduction Project has
begun to reach fulfilment. In 1983, and again in 1984, two pairs laid
eggs but unfortunately none hatched. No less than four clutches were
produced in 1985, and one pair successfully fledged an eaglet – the
first to have been born and bred in Britain for over 70 years. All the
Eyries are strictly protected by wardens of the RSPB and NCC. The
initial failures were due mainly to the age and inexperience of our
released eagles and, in 1985 to the very bad summer.

"The flight of that first young White-tailed Eagle was a
momentous occasion in the species' recolonisation of Britain. More

pairs are continually forming as the released eagles reach maturity. Although importations have now ceased we are confident that enough young will soon be being produced in the wild to ensure the successful return of the White-tailed Eagle to our shores."

John Love was the scientist in charge of this fascinating experiment and his book on the Sea Eagles (see bibliography) is a classic. These islands were an old stronghold of the erne, breeding on Eigg till 1833 (Sgurr) and Cleadale 1877, on Canna to 1875 and in Rhum we read of 8 killed in 1866 and the last pair going in 1907. Rhum, Canna and Eigg all have shearwaters but Rhum's colony is the largest with a third of the world's population.

FORESTATION

The original lower covering of trees was fragmentary even by the early 17th century and virtually extinct until the fine half acre of Beech, Ash and Sycamore standing behind the Post Office (the last building before the Kinloch river) was planted 120 years ago – on the then site of the former Kinloch Lodge which was replaced by the pretentious Castle. The Post Office was the Lodge kitchen originally and has recently been modernised – as have most houses. John Bullough planted about 80,000 trees of various kinds about 70 years ago, and though some failed, and time, neglect and gales have taken their toll, the shores of Loch Scresort and the Castle grounds look naturally and attractively wooded. A small clump of trees (and jungly Rhododendron) at Papadil was for long the only other planting. However, the Nature Conservancy Council have now planted much of the North Side and southwards to Welshman's rock (see the slopes above Kinloch Glen and across the Loch) in a programme of re-establishing the sort of mixed woodland that originally covered the island, mainly of Scots pine, Oak, Rowan, Birch, Aspen and Alder. A shelter belt has been planted to protect the farmland from the prevailing westerlies. Smaller plantations lie above the Harris road near its summit, in the crook of the road twisting down to Harris, and there are plots down Kilmory Glen and Guirdal. Gorse and Broom (for shelter) are planted too, but will decrease as the forest matures. How soil can be restored is seen in a study of worm density: in normal barren heath land there will be one worm per 1 square metre but after a generation of birch growth it is 127 per square metre.

Trees, so often taken for granted, are so easily destroyed, so slow to grow again. (A routine burning blew out of control in Spring 1969 and damaged thousands of young trees on the North Side.) There is a nursery at Kinloch Castle beside the Weather Observation Post and island or West Highland seed is used wherever possible.

In the later 1950's little practical knowledge was available in growing and planting native species, so techniques had to be learnt anew. A steady programme of planting will continue till 1995. From the historical records, peat cores, the relics on Rhum and similar places a picture has now been built up of what original woodland looked like.

Today, on the poorest ground, are planted Birch, Rowan, Hazel and Shrub Willow; on the flushes by the side of burns, Alder and larger Willows; on the dry north and east facing moorlands, Scots Pine; where there are better soils, in more sheltered situations, Oak, Hazel, Wych Elm and Holly; and where there are mineral soils, such as at Guirdil, Ash, Bird Cherry and Hawthorn. This is a simplification and in reality a mixture of those species, and a few more with a restricted distribution, such as Aspen, Gean, Sloe, Guelder-rose and Juniper, are planted. Approaching 1 million trees and shrubs of over 20 species have been planted. This is research which will continue for generations and illustrates the special importance of Rhum; private or commercial forestry interests (who will most benefit) simply could not tackle such researches. Lodgepole pine, Larch, etc., have been used but only as "nursing" shelter to assist the native trees and will be felled when the latter are safely established.

VEGETATION AND FLORA

The main regions correspond to the underlying geological formations. 1. The Torridonian sandstones and shales in north and east. 2. The gabro/ultra-basic central area. 3. The western granophyre (Harris – Orval – A'Bhrideanach triangle). 4. The basalt and limestone to the north west (Fionchra/Monadh Dubh).

Canna to the north west of Rhum is chiefly basalt and in contrast to most of Rhum is a green and fertile island.

Wet heath community is the most abundant formation, over glacial drift, sandstone, shale and acid igneous rocks. There is a main blanket bog area in the centre of the island. The vegetation map gives nine formations. 1. Calluna Heath (granophyre). 2. Wet Heath. 3. Blanket Bog. 4. Nardus Heath (granophyre). 5. Schoenus Fen (where ground water rises from ultra-basic rocks). 6. Molinia Flush (areas enriched by flushing from ground water). 7. Herb-rich Heath.

33

8. Marsh. 9. Agrostis-Festuca Grassland. Man-made plantation now forms a tenth.

About 800 species of Fungi have been recorded, some being new British or even European records and about 90 probably introduced unintentionally with planted hosts.

The flora includes one or two varieties such as Norwegian Sandwort and Alpine Penny Cress. Several species such as Stone Bramble and Scottish Asphodel are unusually numerous and others such as *Saxifraga nivalis* occur outside their usual range. Moss, Campion, Mountain Avens (locally), Mossy Cyphel, Rose-root, Thyme, Mountain Sorrel are common mountain plants, as is Purple Saxifrage, the early flower of damp hanging areas. Natural Bog Myrtle is very rare but has been introduced.

The commonest Flowers can delight. Primroses and attendant Violets can be prolific – even at 1,700 ft. on Hallival or Coire Dubh. On the ridges our smallest "tree" grows – the Least Willow. Both there and on sea rocks there are thrift (Sea Pink) cushions. Fragile Burnett Roses grow on the raised beach at Harris where the flora is almost machair-like. Foxgloves, Wood sorrel and Wild Hyacinth grow both in and out of woodland.

Butterworts (with leaves like stranded starfish) and Sundews are both insect-eating plants. Louse-wort is semi-parasitic on the roots of Heather. Heather only dominates locally as past burning and grazing has reduced it. The slopes are now predominantly grass covered: Purple Moor Grass, Bent and Fescue. Most of the expected plants of the moors are found: Rock Cress, Orchids of several kinds, Blaeberry, Dwarf Juniper, Starry Saxifrage, Cudweed, Bedstraw, Milkwort and Tormentil, Bog Asphodel (latish), various Vetches, Lady's Mantle, Club mosses. "Mire Vegetation" is wide-spread. Puffs of Bog Cotton are attractive. Bog-bean may entirely cover some of the lochans. Forked Spleen-wort and several Rushes and Sedges only occur in one or a few known localities.

Some of the chasms to and beyond Dibidil look like hanging gardens, often wet and lush, with remnants of trees and scrub; the nesting place of many birds.

Altogether more than 2107 kinds of plants have been catalogued. Quite an inventory – and a basis for continual ecological studies. They break down: 905 fungi species, 91 liverwort, 280 mosses, 387 lichens, 3 stoneworts, 42 flowerless herbs (including 28 ferns) and about 400 flowering plants (including 44 grasses, 23 sedges). A vegetation map has now been published, based on field work and air photography.

Orval at the head of Glen Guirdil
Bloodstone Hill, right foreground

GEOLOGY

The main summits to the north of the Harris road are Orval 571m (1,872 ft.), Arn Nev 554m (1,816 ft.), Bloodstone Hill (Creag nan Stardean or Sgor Mhor) 388m (1,273 ft.), Fionchra 447m (1,550 ft.) and Mullach Mor 304m (996 ft.). These are not in the main climbing area. The Cuillin of Rhum, south of the Harris road comprise Barkeval 591m (1,924 ft.), Hallival (Allival) 723m (2,365 ft.), Askival 812m (2,659 ft.) (the island's highest), Trollaval (Trallival or Trallval) 702m (2,300 ft.), Ainshval (Ashval) 781m (2,552 ft.), Sgurr

35

*Askival and Hallival with Askival's prow prominent.
The path to Dibidil can just be made out*

nan Gillean 764m (2,503 ft.), Ruinsival 528m (1,607 ft.), Beinn nan Stac 547m (c.1,850 ft.) and the Prow of Askival – the un-named termination of the East Ridge of that peak.

The North Side, occupying one-sixth of the island is a gentle platform of reddish Torridonian Sandstone, though to the west Orval is in a Granite area. The west-most corner has cliffs rising to nearly 1,000 ft. The Sandstone extends down the east coast as well. It is in fact the southernmost development of the North West Highland facies of these rocks. The only lime-rich ground will be found on Monadh Dubh.

Ainshval – Gillean is Torridonian but overlaid by Felsite and Lewisian Gneiss.

The big central peaks – the climber's peaks – are a complex main centre of Tertiary igneous activity, the wreck of one of the volcanos running up the Atlantic sea-board from Ireland to Greenland. (It extends *downwards* some 44,000 ft.). There is greater development of ultra-basic types here than anywhere else in Britain: Peridotite, Allivalite (named after the peak), Harrisite (after that place),

Eucrite, Gabbro, Granite, Granophyre (in the west), and Felsite. "The Rhum volcano was active no more than 70 million and not less than 25 million years ago" (give or take the odd million years).

Minishal out to Bloodstone Hill are basaltic lava outliers and below the latter can be found Heliotrope, Chalcedony and Agate which have formed in the amygdaloids (vapour cavities in the lava subsequently filling with minerals).

Glacial markings (striae) radiating from the main peaks show Rhum to have had its own ice-cap following the last ice maximum. Coire nan Grunnd contains clear examples of morainal deposits from the peaks above. During the Pleistocene period mainland ice crossed east south east and west north west and erratics of mainland rock are sporadically distributed, particularly on the east coast; even well up on Barkeval and Ard Nev. Granitic screes are conspicuous on Orval. Sron an t-Saighdeir (The Soldier's Nose) summit ridge carries frost stripes and well-developed stone polygons.

The pebble ridge of rounded granite stones along the Harris Bay is an old raised beach and others can be seen at Papadil in the south and Kilmory in the north, at 20, 40 and 100 ft. Kinloch Castle and grounds occupy a large raised beach.

The Mam Lochs area (on the edge of the ultra-basic centre) can be seen clearly from Barkeval; between it and the Kinloch Glen is extremely complex, geologically. There are nearly a score of lochans.

Various papers have been published by the Nature Conservancy Council on the Geology of Rhum. The field guide is on sale at the Rhum office, which also holds many other papers and theses. Research has been going on for a considerable time – MacCulloch published a geological map in 1819. Harker in 1908 published the first major work. Rhum, being special, is much used by students or field parties.

HISTORY

Ptolemy and Tacitus refer to Rhum (calling it Dumna) but its early history is little known until the 18th century. There are few antiquities: an unexplained line of beehive dwellings near Loch Monica, a promontory fort at the foot of Glen Shellesder, 3 Iron Age forts, a bloodstone arrowhead found at Shamhnan Insir, one Norwegian burial cist and a bone ornament from the cave in Bagh na h-Uamha and a few old gravestones in the ruins of a trap for deer can still be made out. Scores of shielings are in evidence and there are two 7th century cross stones. A more recent archaeological story is

The Cross Stone
Bagh na h-Uamha

told below.

Rhum only became part of the Scottish Kingdom in 1266 having been for long under Norwegian dominance. The names point to Norse influence. Papadil is Priest's Valley and Irish records mention a 'Beccan of Rhum' dying in 677.

Clanranald held the island till 1346 when it passed to John of Islay. In 1695 it came into the possession of the MacLeans of Coll who held it for 150 years to sell to the 2nd Marquis of Salisbury in 1845. Campbell of Ormsary had it from 1868-1887.

Dr Johnson (who visited the Hebrides in 1773) has a tale of how the islanders became Protestant. The Laird's sister was a zealous Romanist and thwarted his desire for their conversion. However, he waylaid them one Sunday en route for Mass and a clout or two soon drove them into the kirk, from which they have never left – till the Disruption of 1843 when three-quarters of the people "came out".

Pennant (1772) described how 59 families were living in "nine little hamlets . . . in different places, near which the corn was sown in patches".

In Harris the remains of 30 black houses can still be seen and about 300 acres of ill-named "lazy beds". (The soil gathered into heaped ridges to give depth enough to grow potatoes, barley, oats and kail.)

As man increased, deer decreased. In 1703 Martin Martin reports some hundreds of deer in the mountains. In 1772 Pennant reported 80 deer – and 325 people. In 1796 the human population was 445, in 1871 it was down to 81 and by 1891 only 53 – partly due to a plague of rats which made life unbearable. (One man recorded killing 500 in 1881.)

When cattle prices fell after the Napoleonic Wars Alexander Maclean decided to clear his tenants (they received a year's notice in 1825) and the island was leased to Dr Maclean as a sheepwalk. Fifty people remained and 300 sailed in the *Dove of Harmony* and *Highland Lad* but two years later they and 150 Muck folk also left, in the *St Lawrence*, to Nova Scotia: 71 McKenzies, 44 McLeans, 37 McKays, 20 McMillans, 10 McInnes, 9 McQuarries, 7 McPhadens, 2 McIsaacs, 2 McArthurs, 2 Dalgleish, 2 Stewarts – and 1 Campbell and 1 Cameron. Dr Maclean built Kinloch House and planted the Beeches and Wych Elms we see today but his 8000 sheep were not a success and he emigrated to Australia.

A few years later McLean found he had a dearth of labour so a dozen Skye and Mull crofting families were permitted to settle in the bogs (now the South Wood) along Loch Scresort and out at Port nan Caranean – land useless to sheep – where they eked out an existence that still speaks to us from grey tumbled stones.

Rhum was sold by Alexander's son for conversion to a sporting estate in 1845, the year Hugh Miller visited the island. "There were fields that had borne many a successive harvest, and prostrate cottages, that had been the scenes of christenings, and bridals, and blythe New Year's days – all seemed to bespeak the place a fitting habitation for man; but in the entire prospect not a man nor a dwelling could eye command." The 2nd Marquess of Salisbury stocked the hill with deer and soon conveyed the island to his son, who initiated another clearance to Canada in 1857; one family leaving could trace its ancestry back to 1386. In 1865 Rhum passed to a brother, the Conservative Prime Minister who held it for 4 years before three successive Campbell owners led to its unique spell under the Bulloughs.

Edwin Waugh's book "The Limping Pilgrim on his Wanderings" gives a detailed 99 page description of life on Rhum in the years prior to the Bulloughs. One thing seems not to have changed much:

"The air swarmed with stinging insects; their vindictiveness was something startling. They came down in murderous hordes upon every exposed bit of skin."

It is a pity Waugh had his limp or we would have had an early description of the hills. Some did find their way upwards. The Rev. Dr John Walker reporting on the Hebrides (1764 and 1771) wrote:

"the Remainder, by far the greatest part, may be judged wholly irreclaimable, consisting of steep Mountains, deep Mosses and

Askival and Hallival (with Clough's Crag in front)

Tracks of Land overspread with Rocks . . . It has once been well wooded, and in some of the steep Gullies, inaccessible to cattle, the Oak, the Birch, the Holly and Rowan Tree, are still to be observed growing vigorously.

". . . from this Place, I made a Journey to the highest of these mountains named Ascheval. From the shore we ascended through deep Mosses, whose surface would scarcely carry us, . . . The rest of the Ascent was clambering amidst broken Rocks and falls of water; but among these Rocks, and among the straggling Junipers, I found such a Variety of rare Alpine Plants, as amply requited the Fatigue of the Journey. Some of them, the Inhabitants of the highest Alps in Switzerland, and others of Lapland and Spitsberg."

Timothy Pont in his 17th century map described Rhum as being "steep and wooded mountains" and the Old Statistical Account has it as "the Kingdom of the Wild Forest". Maybe it will come again. It was reported to James VI as "an isle of small profit" and perhaps its poorness helped it to escape much of the clan and dynastic feuding that destroyed so much elsewhere. No news was probably good news for its poor inhabitants.

In 1887 the estate, advertised in *The Times*, was bought by John Bullough, a Lancashire industrialist and inventor of cotton-spinning machinery, who had already fallen for sporting Scotland and bought Meggernie Castle in Glen Lyon. His father, James Bullough, had been a weaver at the age of 7 but an inventive talent had seen him rise to prosperous security. John, who took the firm's fortunes to their peak, was "canny" and loved Rhum for its peace and quiet, a contrast to business and politics. He stayed in the old Kinloch House (the present Post Office was part of it) and died in 1891.

His son George had been packed off on a world tour that year (perhaps showing too great an interest in a youthful stepmother) and his love of Rhum was marked by a brash ostentation. He came back laden with treasures from the east and decided to build a real castle on Rhum. No expense was spared. The workmen, from Lancashire, were duly supplied with kilts – an were no doubt to make acquaintance with the midges. The red sandstone was shipped block by block from Arran in the Clyde and the soil for gardens and trees came from Ayrshire. Grapes and peaches could be grown in the greenhouses, venison was ready on the hill, there were fish for the taking, even a turtle pond, rose and Italian gardens – with fourteen gardeners! The castle was supplied with every "mod con", the laundry was discreetly situated at Kilmory, eight miles off, the first home electrical generator was installed from the Allt Slugan (1898 – and some houses were only rewired by the Nature Conservancy Council over 50 years later). Work involving the diversion of the Kilmory and Long Loch waters to the Kinloch River was continued to improve the fishings. The population rose to about 100, just to keep one family comfortable on their periodic visits. The building is so outrageously out of place that Sir John Betjeman called it "the stone embodiment of good King Edward's reign". While Derek Cooper commented, "It is rather like observing a vision of St Pancras Station in the middle of the Sinai Desert". It had its days of glory. The Bullough yacht *Rhouma* was used as a hospital ship in the Boer War, earning its owner his knighthood, and eventually sold to the Italians.

Then came the First World War and its aftermath. In 1936 there were only 20 inhabitants – and another war looming. Sir George ("Seoras") died in 1939 and in 1957 his widow, Lady Bullough sold the estate to the Nature Conservancy Council. As W. H. Murray says, by the end of the war the Castle had become a bit of a pink elephant.

Over at Harris a tile vault was built, bits of which still show on the bank behind the lodge, but later a family mausoleum was constructed in the style of a Greek temple. Here in 1967, Monica, Lady Bullough, was laid to rest, the last link with the old days. She was 98 when she died.

Hallival, Trollaval and Ainshval from Harris.
The Bullough Mausoleum in the foreground

There has been some recovery in population since the Nature Conservancy Council took over, numbers being between 30 and 40 with up to 10 pupils at the school, which also doubles as church. The school teacher is the only resident not employed by the Nature Conservancy Council. Secondary education has to be continued on the mainland, at Fort William. The nearest resident doctor is on Eigg, the nearest dentist or hospital, Fort William. It is not all desert island bliss, though hardly likely to produce the tragedy recounted on a Kilmory gravestone erected by Murdo Matheson in memory of his beloved children: Rebecca 17, John 12, Christina Ann 8, Murdo 6, William John 4, and Archibald Duncan 7 months, "all of which died of diphtheria between the 7th and 9th of September, 1873". (Murdo Matheson took the well used road to the North American continent where his descendants still live).

Lord Salisbury in 1847, possibly to give employment during the potato famine, attempted to divert the waters of the Long Loch and upper Kilmory into the Kinloch by a dam forming the "New Loch" – which broke two days after completion. A cutting instead leads the Long Loch waters to the Kinloch, and in 1891 the Kilmory was tapped. However, the Kinloch never has been the salmon river envisaged. The scheme was abandoned and some of the original flow restored.

The island is very much a laboratory – as well as being a museum (rare and interesting plants and insects, the unique Shearwater colony, etc). Its past history of innate poverty of soil, destruction of forest cover, over-grazing, indiscriminate burning and over-population is that of much of the Highlands and islands. If restoration research bears fruit here, this will be of value everywhere else. Work is linked with similar efforts in other Reserves. Research and educational opportunities will play an ever-increasing part in the years ahead.

For an interesting account of the island's history the booklet by John Love is worth purchasing (see bibliography). He quotes John MacCulloch (1824), a passage which shows how ideas about a place can change – or do they?

"There is a great deal of stormy magnificence about the lofty cliffs, as there is generally all round the shores of Rum; and they are, in most places, as abrupt as they are inaccessible from the sea. The interior is one heap of rude mountains, scarcely possessing an acre of level land. It is the wildest and most repulsive of all islands. The outlines of Hallival and Haskeval are indeed elegant and render the island a beautiful and striking object from the sea . . . If it is not

Bloodstone Hill, Rhum

always bad weather in Rum, it cannot be good very ofter

In 1983 a field behind the farm was being ploughed deeper than before and stone flakes and an arrowhead were turned up. An emergency dig was undertaken and in the next three years tens of thousands of flakes and chippings and tons of samples have been collected. Burnt hazelnuts made it possible to carbon date the site which turned out to be the earliest known (Mesolithic) settlement in Scotland – 8,500 years old! Rock for arrowheads was brought from Bloodstone Hill, worked here, and exported (the stone is easily recognisable and arrowheads have been found up and down the west coast), but it may be that this was a more permanent settlement as well as a knapping floor. This is only 2,000 years after the last ice age and a fascinating discovery. Caroline Wickham-Jones has led the investigations and the accounts mentioned in the bibliography make interesting reading. Rhum has again proved special.

VOLUNTARY WORKING

Free bothy accommodation is offered in return for voluntary help in conservation and general estate work on the island. Four days 'on' and three 'off' are normal. Apply to the Chief Warden for details. Rhum offers a wide scope for studies of all kinds. School and college parties are welcomed, and private projects can often be set up. Any help, amateur or professional is welcomed. One of the joys of Rhum is seeing plenty of human activity on a remote Hebridean Island. Whether planting trees, repairing roads or pursuing specialist studies in botany, geology or ornithology, the island gives plenty of interest.

FISHING

Some sea fishing and loch fishing for brown trout only is permitted. Details and permits can be obtained from the Reserve Office on arrival.

Mark Richards 1986

Hallival and Askival

Part Two: Mountaineering

GUIDELINES

Climbing parties should number between 4 and 15 and should apply to the Chief Warden, through their club secretaries, for permission to climb and to arrange dates. On Rhum an eye should be kept on the map board outside The White House as this shows day to day restrictions. When work demands it the whole island is closed to visitors. The Kilmory area is only open on Sundays. Collecting rocks, plants, antlers, etc., is not allowed. "Gardening" of routes and the use of pitons should be avoided and it is easiest to discuss plans with the Chief Warden. These rules apply for the safety of both visitors and environment. There is no rescue service on Rhum and only a limited amount of equipment available at the Reserve office. One benefit of these regulations is a real feeling of uncluttered remoteness. You just won't meet other people or queue for a route or see distasteful litter and erosion. Rhum is a rather special place and it is desirable that it stays so for future generations.

HILL WALKING

Wandering on Rhum is seldom other than rough or wet – frequently both together. Walkers should have proper boots and take more than usual care.

The paths mentioned previously are all excellent for walking and the coastal circuit from Kinloch to Dibidil to Harris, and back is a worthwhile excursion. Glen Dibidil has a character all of its own, and has been compared with Glen Sannox in Arran. The passes at its head, and the Bealach Barkeval are good routes to Harris. Coire nan Grunnd and Bagh na h-Uamha (Bay of the cave) are worth visiting.

There are two nature trails starting at the pier. One path runs up the Kinloch Glen for a couple of miles, the other wends out to the shielings at Port nan Caranean by the most easterly point of Rhum. All paths shown on the 1:50,000 map do exist but in both cases 'Nature Trail' has been indicated incorrectly, one being simply the track to Dibidil, the other a largely abandoned track up the north side of the Kinloch Glen. The track through to Glen Shellesder is pleasant and leads to an impressive bit of coastline with a waterfall,

A waterfall beside the path from Kinloch to Dibidil

From Beinn nan Stac: left to right -
Sgurr nan Gillean, Ruinsval and Trollaval at the head of Glen Dibidil,
Askival and, just showing, Hallival and the Prow of Askival

promontory fort and natural arch all close together. The path continues to Guirdil (bothy on the shore) with a fine view of Bloodstone Hill. From the centre of the island a path follows up a stream (actually a cutting, see below) through the Monadh Mhiltich to the Bealach a' Bhraigh Bhig between the ragged bastion of Orval and flower-ringed Fionchra. It drops a little and then traverses under Orval (its notable pinnacle is well seen) to the wide Bealach an Dubh-bhraigh before wending up to Bloodstone Hill. The path skirts a hollow at the end to disappear down onto the seaward face. Both in prehistoric times and last century bloodstone was extracted. The summit is a cliff-edge perch of some character. There is no path through Glen Guirdil but it is an easy line of travel, up or down, and can link up with the Shellesder path. The road down to Kilmory should only be followed on Sunday, when it is recommended. There is a superb sandy bay, much appreciated by resident children and visitors alike for Sunday trips on a sunny day. The deer on Rhum have worn tracks, often in likely places like below crags, and these are worth using as the going is never easy on the island and, on lower slopes especially, can be purgatorial in the rank growth.

In the Salisbury and later era attempts were made to catch the upper waters of the Kilmory river and lead them into the Kinloch River. This accounts for the various cuttings and dams visible where the roads and rivers all criss-cross in the middle of the island. The major dam collapsed as soon as completed so the scheme never really functioned as planned. You can amuse yourself on a wet day trying to trace it all on the ground. The 1:50,000 doesn't really indicate much of it.

THE MAIN RIDGES TRAVERSE

This is nowhere comparable to Skye and only mild scrambling is called for, apart possibly for one step, which is more tedious to avoid than difficult to climb – yet these ridges combine to give a splendid day's walking.

A start is usually made on Barkeval (from Coire Dubh) or direct to Hallival. The central ridge from Hallival to Askival has an unusually airy grass rooftop (where shearwater skulls, the remains of eagles' eating, can sometimes be seen) – and the Askival "Pinnacle". This is in fact a slab step and is not difficult, though the walker may find it impressive from below. It can be skirted on the east and Askival may be missed out entirely by traversing the western scree slopes to the Bealach an Oir.

The summit of Askival, Rhum's highest at 812m, 2,663 ft, has a commanding view: the Skye Cuillin and Red Hills to the north while the roll call of mainland lies eastwards: Kintail, Knoydart, Morar, Moidart – to Ardnamurchan Point, beyond which Ben More in Mull is prominent. In every direction there is a scattering of islands and below the sunset runs the Outer Hebrides. No inland mountain view can rival this western combination of sky, sea and blue peaks.

Askival's West Ridge is descended to the Pass of Gold, Bealach an Oir, and Trollaval, then the Bealach an Fhuaran (Pass of the Springs) demarcates the group of Ainshval-Sgurr nan Goibhrean – Sgurr nan Gillean, which are no longer gabbro-like in character.

It is possible to continue west along the Leac a' Chaisteil to Ruinsival and Harris or to drop down to Dibidil or, from either, to take road or path back to the start. The former is considerably longer. It is also possible to return to the last bealach, skirt Trollaval to the Bealach an Oir and home by skirting under Askival and Hallival (The Atlantic corrie of Glen Harris). The South Ridge of Askival – for Beinn nan Stac – is harder than anything mentioned

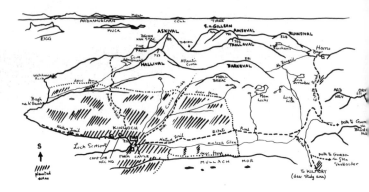

above, but can be crossed from the Bealach an Oir and a wide shelf followed over the East Prow of Askival to Coire nan Grunnd and the Allt na h-Uamha for Kinloch. A hundred years ago a family living at Papadil lodged their son at Kinloch for his schooling during the week. Each Saturday the 14-year-old walked home, each Sunday he returned to Kinloch. Makes it a bit difficult to complain does it not?

ROCK-CLIMBING

GRADINGS follow the normal descriptive system. "Severe" may cover quite a range, from mild severe to hard severe in some cases. "Very Severes" are few as yet. Right and left are always given as facing the crag.

In this revision these gradings have been left unaltered though in a few harder new climbs modern gradings are used as submitted. Distances are given, in feet as few people think in metres as yet. Heights of summits etc are shown in metres to allow easy use of the Ordnance Survey map.

DESCRIPTIONS have given difficulties on every single crag; many were not even resolved by visits by Anne Littlejohn and Hamish Brown. This has mainly been due to duplications of climbs, to original poor descriptions, the multiplication of differing names for features and the mixing up of the many Upper, Middle, Bottom, Lower, and what-have-you, Tiers. From this editor's nightmare we now have a definitive guide which climbers will be able to use profitably.

HISTORICAL It is impossible to tell who first ventured along the main ridges. The climbers began to arrive in the 1890's; very much

THE CLIMBING AREAS MAIN CRAGS NUMBERED

1. *Barkeval, South Crags*
2. *Hallival S.E. Face*
3. *Clough's Crag*
4. *Coire nan Grundd Crags*
5. *N.E. Face of Askival*
6. *Trollaval, Harris Buttress*
7. *Ruinsival's Tiers*

the era of the landed gentry like Sir Hugh Munro himself who in Vol. I of the Scottish Mountaineering Club Journal describes a traverse of Hallival and Askival. Raeburn, Bell, Brown and other SMC stalwarts were active, writing delightfully of impossibly precipitous places, which they proceeded to climb up – and down. In Vol. X, Harker gives the first 'guidebook'. The first World War altered the scene and visits were only made again in the thirties by the Oxbridge fraternity who were the first, if tentatively, to climb rock for its own sake: Hallival 1932, 33, Askival Slab 1937. E. W. Hodge gave a resume in the SMC Jubilee Journal, 1939.

It was only after the Second War that democracy began to assert itself. The Junior Mountaineering Club of Yorkshire discovered Ruinsival, the Edinburgh University climbers visited Askival's North West Crags, the Triangular Buttress, Giant's Staircase. The next year W. H. Murray and M. Ward climbed Archangel and Dan Stewart and Donald Bennet added routes in the west. The 1948 SMC Journal had another 'guide' to the then known routes, well produced by J. G. Parish. Apart from some good routes added to Harris Buttress the fifties saw little activity.

However, in 1959 Anne Littlejohn began a decade of visits with various partners and has probably climbed more extensively on the island than anyone. Her parties, the groups with H. Brown and J. Matyssek, and Ian Clough and his clients were all regular visitors in the later sixties. Only a few good routes have been added since despite there being plenty of scope. The Orval Pinnacle has provided some fun but climbing on the northern side and sea cliffs is not encouraged.

BARKEVAL, 1924 ft.

Barkeval is the best viewpoint for seeing the main peaks and worth a visit for this alone. The climbing is not visible from the eastern approaches, being on the south side, and is better than once thought. The crags can be reached in an hour from Kinloch by going up the Coire Dubh path to the Bealach Barkeval and over the summit; or simply up Glen Harris if coming from the west.

To descend from the summit, go east about 30 yards where two cairns line down to the top of Honeycomb Arête, which gives an easy scramble. This arête is separated east of Narnia Arête by a V-gully. Narnia Arête is useful for a quick ascent.

Barkeval is "the most extensive mass of peridotite in Britain, perhaps the best rock in the world for climbing" (Harker). It is certainly unusual!

SOUTH CRAGS

From below, a big overhang, just west of the summit, is seen above a wide scooped gully, usually referred to as the "Waterslide". This vanishes at the foot of the top rocks but becomes the main scree and grass shoot running right down into Glen Harris. Left of the Waterslide lies Western Isles Buttress; right the big, broken Broad Buttress, then a gully, then the distinctive Narnia Arête, the V-Gully, and Honeycomb Arête. These ribs join at the top corner of the Rectangle to form the long West Edge which drops well down into the glen. East again the East Edge drops down similarly. (These edges should give climbs.)

Left again of Western Isles Buttress is a conspicuous Green Patch: Rose Root passes west of it and Rangail west again. Beyond that the crags are too broken, as everywhere else on this hill.

On Broad Buttress, Barkeval

The convenient starting point is the grass/scree Rectangle below Broad Buttress.

Western Isles Buttress. 350 ft. Diff. J. Matyssek. 18.5.67. The buttress left of the waterslide. Start at cairn, top left of the Rectangle and follow best line.

Rose-Root Slab and Crack. 260 ft. Severe. J. Matyssek, H. Brown, I. Moreland. 18.5.67. West of Western Isles is a bay with a 60 ft. slab to left. Climb it and 20 ft. on in same line to an overhanging nook. Break right over this to grassy ledges just left of the green Patch. Right up small slab under a face to base of deeply-cut chimney, 50 ft., crux. From stony shelf above finish straight up for about 60 ft.

Broad Buttress. 400 ft. Mod. J. Matyssek, H. Cook. 22.5.67. The buttress whose base forms the top of the Rectangle. Can be climbed anywhere.

Narnia Arête. 350 ft. Mod. The conspicuous arête east of Broad Buttress. Keep to the crest and enjoy the peculiar rock!
   Beyond this again is a V-shaped gully and the easy Honeycomb Arête, see above.

Black and Tan. 170 ft. Mild Severe. C. Ross, A. J. Young. 28.5.75. Well up the gully between Broad Buttress and Narnia Arête (cairn). Climb a black, streaked slab to a corner with a grass ledge and poor belay (55 ft.). Take the paler slab above, crux at start, to good stance 6 ft. down past the top (70 ft.). Follow slab and corner above to cairn (45 ft.).

Christopher. 140 ft. Severe. H. Brown, C. Ross. 28.5.75. On the gully wall of Broad Buttress. Gain a chimney and follow this to ledge (45 ft.). Move up right, then exposed step up and left (crux), to follow crack then chimney, ending high on Broad Buttress (95 ft.).

Aficionado. 165 ft. Severe. D. Bearhop, A. McClintock. 30.3.82. The wide gully to the right of Honeycomb Arête has a small subsidiary gully on its left with a chimney at the back. The route takes the prominent crack running up the right slab from this subsidiary gully. At 85 ft. a large overhang niche is reached – belay. Take the overhang direct. The angle eases thereafter and an obvious intrusive band of rock is followed as it traverses round to finish on easier

On the first ascent of Black & Tan, Barkeval
ground (80 ft.).

Rangail Route. Severe. I. Southern, H. Brown, W. Harrison. 27.6.71. Left of the Rectangle, follow to west end of the protruding band of dark gravelly rock. Cairn below an obvious prow, just right of a trap fault. Climb the prow, 60 ft. to easy ground. Beyond, a trap fault is seen rising from a black and grassy bay. Climb the steep rib to the right of the bay, crux at top where it overhangs slightly. 85 ft. This leads to a maze of ribs, wee wa's and honeycomb rock giving 200 ft. of scrambling.

HALLIVAL, 2365 ft.

From Kinloch approach either by the Bealach Barkeval or by the Dibidil path as far as the Allt Mor na h-Uamha where it is easy to break up to the north east flank. The **North Ridge**, really N.N.W., presents no difficulty other than optional scrambling on the top steps (150 ft. Mod.) which can be turned by gully on right. To the left the north east flank offers easy gullies and chimneys though the 1932 explorers were impressed by overhanging buttresses which might repay investigation. **The East Ridge** is about V. Diff. and forms the

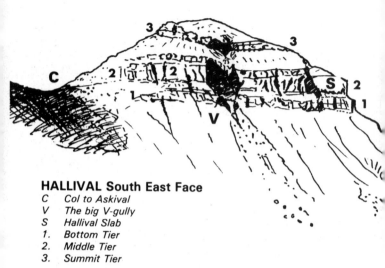

HALLIVAL South East Face

C   *Col to Askival*
V   *The big V-gully*
S   *Hallival Slab*
1.   *Bottom Tier*
2.   *Middle Tier*
3.   *Summit Tier*

skyline as seen from Askival. Its history is vague but probably dates from the same party. The crags have been formed by bands of allivalite and peridotite. The climbing is generally sound. The upper slopes are littered with large chunky boulders, as an old S.M.C. Journal puts it: "scattered about in the most promiscuous manner." The climbing lies on the South East Face overlooking Coire nan Grunnd and is most easily reached from Kinloch by traversing round the foot of the East Ridge. Some other descents on the face are mentioned in the descriptions of climbs. There are three obvious tiers: The Summit Tier, and the Middle and Bottom Tiers. The foot of climbs can be reached in 1½-2 hours from Kinloch.

SUMMIT TIER
Stands well back from the top of the Middle Tier and is only about 40 ft. high at the south west (left) end, diminishing to a rocky step above the Hallival Slab.

MIDDLE TIER
This is the main line of crags and runs from the East Ridge to the Askival-Hallival col, divided for convenience into three sections.
1. Right Section. The very conspicuous Hallival Slab, over 100 ft.

The Prow, Askival and Hallival from Bagh na h-Uamha

wide, which leans back above an overhanging base and the rocks to the East Ridge. (Oxford Groove at the right end in fact cuts through both Middle and Bottom Tiers.)

2. Central Section. From the gully bounding Hallival Slab, the range of ribs as far as the big scooped V-gully; this gully in fact runs down through all three tiers and far down into Coire nan Grunnd as a long scree tongue.

3. Left Section. From the big V-gully to the Askival col.

BOTTOM TIER

A more broken line offering climbing only below Oxford Groove and the Hallival Slab, where in fact there are good, clean routes of up to 80 ft. The Tier is separated from the Middle Tier by a steeply-sloping ledge of grass and scree.

Below the Bottom Tier, at the right, there is a certain amount of rock banding, too broken up to offer good climbing. The following route goes up the most continuous piece of rock, a blunt rib with a slabby right wall. As it lies directly below Oxford Groove it can be an interesting approach to the crags.

Hallival

Choochter Rib. 200 ft. V. Diff. I. Clough, K. Ross. 22.5.67. Start from the lowest rocks and keep close to rib. Climb 10 ft. slab on right, gain shelf on left and mantleshelf onto flake on nose, An awkward move lands one on a ledge in an overhanging recess, belay 60 ft. A short chimney then right and up crest, 50 ft. Climb ridge above.

SUMMIT TIER
Frustration. 50 ft. Severe. J. Matyssek, H. Brown. 19.5.67. The first obvious double-decker incut corner on the tier; right of the top of the escape route from the V-gully. Climb the corners.

Corner Crack. 25 ft. Severe. M. McCallum, A. Littlejohn. 31.8.66. Above Ashes: the tier is cut by an obvious steep corner. Scramble from a cairn and climb the corner. Small block at top is firm, or step left to avoid it.

Oxford Groove. 200 ft. Severe. R. Low, M. Nettleton, A. Cunliffe, F. Pullinger. 1933. The obvious groove that cleaves both Bottom and Middle Tiers, immediately south of the East Ridge.

MIDDLE TIER
Thumbs. 70 ft. Hard Severe. A. Nisbet, S. R. Bateson 10.4.74. The smaller groove right of Oxford Groove. Climb it, passing a pinnacle

at 20 ft.

Cambridge Arête. 75 ft. Severe. A. Parker, J. Young. The arête immediately left of the Middle Tier section (i.e., the top half) of Oxford Groove. Up blocks left of overhang, then deep 12 ft. groove, and traverse to arête which is followed for 40 ft. to finish by an awkward crack.

Red Brick. 70 ft. Diff. E. Nisbet, A. Littlejohn. 19.5.61. Start as for Cambridge Arête, but instead of traversing right, traverse left on to the edge of the Allival Slab. Up edge for a few feet, then slant left up an obvious series of ledges to finish easily beside the top of the Camb. Arête.

Flake and Crack Route. 115 ft. V. Diff. 19.6.66. J. Matyssek, H. Brown and party. A third of the way along under the overhangs of the Allival Slab there is a corner where a climb up right to a big flake leads onto the Slab above and a good finish straight up it to an obvious steep crack.

Hallival Slab. This is bounded on the left by a gully giving an uninteresting climb, but a 25 ft. crack in its right wall gives access to the Bottom left corner of the Slab. A. Littlejohn describes two lines, about 150 ft., Diff. An easy rising traverse leads to the top right corner of the Slab, whence a short steep crack in the wall above leads to the crest of the East Ridge, cairn, some 20 yds. left of the top of Ox Groove. Alternatively the slab may be traversed at a lower level until it becomes steep with small holds and fine exposures. Up and slightly right to the end at top of Ox Groove. See also Flake and Crack, above.

Helen's Horror. 150 ft. Diff. M. McCallum, H. Steven. 28.8.66. About 25 ft. left of the Allival Slab is a deep trap chimney. Climb this by bridging. At overhang, awkward step right, then up grass and easy rock to small cave. Leave this by crawling along a small ledge on the right and then up a short wall.

Asphodel. 160 ft. V.S. A. Littlejohn, M. McCallum. 31.8.66. (Crack inspected with top rope). Round the corner to the left of Allival Slab are three deep grooves. This is the middle one, 100 ft. or so left of Helen's Horror. Traverse onto the arête on the right, then follow a slanting crack to the foot of a vertical 15 ft. crack in the right wall.

Climb this strenuously to good finishing holds on the right and continue to a stance among piled blocks, 110 ft. Continue up a crack formed by two of the blocks to a rocky hollow. Finish up a crack directly ahead, passing an overhanging block on the left.

Lotus. 210 ft. M. Severe. M. McCallum, A. Littlejohn. 30.8.66. The leftmost of the three grooves mentioned above. At 25 ft. avoid an overhang on the right and at the top traverse left by a rocky ramp and go up into an amphitheatre of loose earth and rocks. Finish by traversing piled blocks to the right and climbing the second groove beyond or, better (Hard Severe, A.L.) by a layback crack immediately above the line of the groove.

Ashes. 90 ft. V. Diff. A. Littlejohn, M. McCallum. 30.8.66. The Central Section is divided by two streams. A few yards to the left of the right-hand-stream climb a steep groove with an overhang about three-quarters height.

Descent line. Just left of Ashes it is possible to climb down. Diff. at most. Start at large block at top of gully, cairn, bear left, then right. Steep at foot, but good spike at 15 ft.

Amaranth. 95 ft. Severe. A. Littlejohn, M. McCallum. 31.8.66. This good line lies several buttresses to the right of the big V-gully. A crack runs up the middle of a wall which is set back in the crags. A small projecting block in the crack makes it unmistakable. Start at a small cave, cairn, beside arête right of line of easy slabs. Climb overhang and small slab then easily to ledge below crack. Follow the crack up the wall, past projecting block, to finish just right of triangular recess containing a square block.

Moly. 95 ft. V. Diff. A. Littlejohn, M. McCallum. 23.8.66. A wide, obvious groove situated centrally in the Left Section beyond the V-gully. Start by a trap dyke behind a flake on the right wall, step into the groove about 20 ft. up and when groove becomes a deep crack take the chimney on the right. This has a loose protruding flake at the bottom, more large blocks and a capstan above.

Midge. 90 ft. V. Diff. M. McCallum, A. Littlejohn. 22.8.66. 200 ft. right of the South Ridge of Allival climb a vee-groove with an obliquely-jammed block half way up and a large square-cut overhang at the top – which is avoided on the left.

Midgeless. 65 ft. Diff. M. McCallum, A. Littlejohn. 23.8.66. Fifty feet left of Midge: a steep corner crack with an awkward finish on the right.

The big-V-gully is NOT an easy route of ascent or descent. Beyond it, for the Left Section it is as quick to use the South Ridge as to try and descend. However, from the gully it is possible to bear right over easy slabs and to gain a green gully which breaks up to the top of the Tier.

BOTTOM TIER

Breeze. 65 ft. Severe. J. Matyssek, H. Brown. 22.5.67. The right wall of the lower section of Oxford Groove is a smooth slab which breaks into cracks higher up. Start at the extreme right and climb straight up.

Easy ascent/descent can be made up the Bottom and Middle Tiers by the gully marking the left end of the Allival Slab, and by the traversing lines described on the slab. (see above).

Gargoyle Chimney. 80 ft. Severe. J. Matyssek, H. Brown and party. 19.6.66. The next chimney left of Oxford Groove. A conspicuous chockstone sticks out at the foot. Pull over this 'gargoyle' and up the chimney. This makes a good start to the Cambridge Arête above.

Diamond Corner. 70 ft. Hard Severe. J. Matyssek, H. Brown. 19.5.67. Twenty-five feet left of Gargoyle a groove with a diamond-shaped overhang. Cairn. Up the corner, pass overhang to right, bear left to crest above it and climb to top.

Haddie. 60 ft. Severe. S. R. Bateson, T. Little. 8.4.74. The obvious line up the wall left of Diamond Corner. Start at a sentry box and follow the crack.

Relish. 65 ft. HVS. G. Nicoll, J. Banks. 5.5.84. Climb the rib between Gargoyle Chimney and Oxford Groove in a wall and obvious crack above.

Salad Days. 80 ft. VS. G. Nicoll, J. Banks. 5.5.84. Start 13 ft. right of Diamond Corner, up a steep cracked wall to blocks then traverse 6 ft. right and climb corners to the top.

Sunny Side. 70 ft. Severe. J. Matyssek, H. Brown. 19.5.67. Forty-five feet left of Diamond Corner beyond grassy gully; cairned start in centre of wall almost under overhanging prow. Up to pedestal, on to pock-marked band to bear left a few feet and on up crack slightly right. Fine clean rock.

ASKIVAL, 2659 ft.

Askival is the highest point of the island and a magnificent viewpoint. It also has a certain amount of climbing on every side. The North Ridge is the finest section of all the Rhum ridges, the East Ridge is easy, if steep; there is a series of ribs between it and the ridge down to the Beinn an Stac col – the South, and hardest of the easy main ridges. There is an area of rock on its flank and then the south west is mainly boulders and scree. The West Ridge to Bealach an Oir presents easy scrambling near the top which can be avoided by keeping to the south; while between it and the North Ridge lies the North West Face with some of the steepest good gabbro on Rhum. All these easy lines will present no difficulty to competent hillwalkers: early writings tend to make them sound more difficult.

THE NORTH RIDGE

This was climbed by Munro in the last decade of the last century and may have been traversed locally before that by estate staff if not earlier still. Old S.M.C. Journals have interesting descriptions. The ridge gives about 600 ft. of scrambling with the one steeper slabby step, the so-called, Pinnacle. This gives a 30-ft. climb, moderate – as is the gully by-passing it on the west. The easy bypass is on the east. This ridge has a steep west flank which should yield routes. Access is difficult. One route is recorded:

Zig Zag. 120 ft. Severe. J. Matyssek, H. Brown. 19.6.66. After climbing the Pinnacle the ridge levels for a bit. At the next steepening descend the gully to the west (right). Facing the ridge again, the route goes up the buttress to the right (south), ending on top of the step. Start at the lowest rocks by right-bearing cracks to avoid overhang. Break up and traverse left to climb up edge of gully to stance at the end of a ledge. Either climb the groove above or follow the ledge right until it is possible to climb up. Continue to the top of the step.

THE EAST RIDGE

First climbed by J. H. Bell and W. Brown at Easter 1897. All

Askival over the Bealach an Oir

difficulties can be avoided but more sporting variations are there for the taking. The ridge steepens near the top and a teeter over a jammed block leads to a sandy shoulder a bit below and north of the summit.

SOUTH EAST FACE

This breaks up into a number of ridges all ending on the small summit plateau. Various routes cannot be placed here due to poor descriptions. The climbing is good, however.

Ogilvie's Ridge. Diff. I. Ogilvie, J. Ward, P. Holloway. 28.6.38. South of the East Ridge is a shallow gully and beyond this and about a third of the way across the face is a steep, well-defined ridge. Good steep rock. About half way up, 15 ft. short of the top of a 70 ft. chimney finish right on a steep, exposed slab. Narrow pinnacle above climb on right to neck beyond. Cross, 25 ft., along the exposed edge and traverse several easy pinnacles to finish about 40 yds. from the summit cairn. (Search has failed to locate this route.).

Askival pinnacle   Photo by Donald J.Bennet

Rouma Route. V. Diff. This is probably a variation to Ogilvie's Route of 1938, but as the line of that route is uncertain, the following description is appended.

South of the East Ridge are some scree filled gullies, beyond which lies a prominent slab split by a chimney (cairn).

Climb the chimney or harder, the slab, and two small steps leading to a steepening (80 ft.). A chimney above leads to a serrated crest with an unclimbed vertical step (70 ft.). Ogilvie turned this on the right, but better is either of two corners to the left. If the first corner on the left is taken it should be left before it ends to step right onto a narrow crest which ends the route. Scrambling lands one about 40 ft. along from the summit of Askival.

Parish, 1948, mentions a slab on the flank of the **South Ridge.** This easy ridge drops down to run out to Beinn nan Stac, the Dibidil face of which can offer evening entertainment to bothy dwellers.

THE PROW OF ASKIVAL

The East Ridge of Askival continues out eastwards to form a very definite PROW which is well seen from the South of Rhum as one approaches the island. It is not named on the map. North of the Prow lies Coire nan Grunnd and south, Coire nan Stac. Above these corries are two lines of crags running out from the Prow; at about the 1,500 ft. level, often below clouds in bad conditions.

CLOUGH'S CRAG

(The south east crags of Askival Prow.) These extend for at least half a mile looking down into Coire nan Stac. They are in two well-defined tiers on the long, right portion, while left, south, they jut forward in a big bulge of rock before a definite break where there is a grass slope with a burn coming down. Beyond the break the crags continue – so far unexplored. Most routes have been well marked and described:

Consolation Crack. 65 ft. Diff. A. Littlejohn, E. Nisbet. 18.5.61. At the extreme right end of the crags are two small buttresses, the right one having several conspicuous overhangs in its upper portion. To the left of this buttress is a large grassy bay. Start at the top of this bay. A rough slab on the right leads to a ledge from whose left end a steep 25 ft. crack leads to the top.

Right-Hand Buttress, Direct. 80 ft. V.S. (Crux first inspected with top rope.) A. Littlejohn, E. Nisbet. 18.5.61. Starts at cairn at the bottom right hand corner of the frontal wall. Traverse left at first, then straight up to awkward position close under the overhangs. Move delicately left (Crux) to reach a large slab. Belay high on left.

Recross slab to right and finish by steep 20 ft. corner.

Dribble. 130 ft. V. Diff. I. Clough. 24.5.67. About 50 yards left of Right-Hand Buttress. Cairn and arrow marks start of an obvious corner; probably wet, normally.

Eyrie Arête. 130 ft. V. Diff. I. & N. Clough, K. Ross. 24.5.67. Cairn and arrow start, about 40 ft. left of Dribble. Climb slabs and crack on right flank of arête to small overhung ledge. Round arête and climb to grass ledge and block belay, 80 ft. Go right and climb left-slanting gangway to top.

Satisfaction. 80 ft. Very Severe. D. Bearhop, A. Tibbs. 29.3.82. Twenty feet right of Eyrie Arête there is another prominent ridge. Traverse onto the ridge from the right-hand side and climb onto arête (crux). Move up the arête until a good block is obtained. Move back right and take up the obvious line, finishing by a prominent hand-wide crack.

The Candle. 140 ft. M. Severe. I. Clough, K. Ross. 26.5.67. A short distance left of Eyrie a tall pillar is set in a niche in the wall. Climb the left crack of the candle to its top, move right and climb crack to a ledge, belay, 70 ft. Obvious corner directly above was avoided by climbing left to a grass terrace, 70 ft. The Upper Tier continuation gives 100 ft. of Diff. climbing. On the Upper Tier, above Right-Hand Buttress, are two routes up twin buttresses, separated by a grass gully:–

Amble Arête. 100 ft. Mod. N. Clough, K. Ross. 24.5.67. Climb the right hand twin up the crest on good holds.

The Ramp. 100 ft. V. Diff. I. Clough. 24.5.67. The left twin, up the ramp, then right and climb crest.

Both starts cairned.

The following routes are on the bulging buttress just before, and right of, the break in the cliffs.

Trap Chimney. 190 ft. Diff. I. Clough, J. Greenwood. 26.5.67. Cairn, arrow marked start of obvious trap chimney near right of buttress. Climb chimney to ledge on left, 60 ft. Continue up the fault, passing under two large chokestones.

Fluch. 200 ft. V. Diff. I. Clough, K. Ross. 24.5.67. About 30 ft. left of Trap Chimney: start, cairn, below big corner. Strenuous crack to ledge, belay, 40 ft. Continue up corner to reach belay on grass ledge under twin cracks, 70 ft. Take right crack. Climb up into bay on left, 50 ft. and corner to top.

Fuarr. 210 ft. Diff. J. Greenwood, N. Clough. 24.5.67. Arrow at start, 30 ft. left of Fluch. Up slab to corner. Climb right hand crack to large grass ledge, belay, 100 ft. Above, trend leftwards over slabs.

Gemme. 300 ft. V. Diff. D. Goldie, S. Pearson, R. Pitt, D. Forrest. April 1980. Start: far left of lower tier route marked by arrow (up crack) 15 ft. to left of this climb slab to arrow on right wall. Climb crack up wall to grass ledge. 2. Climb steep slab. 3. Short traverse left to slab and climb to top of tier.

COIRE NAN GRUNND CRAGS

(The north east crags of Askival Prow.) These overlook the loch in a long escarpment, giving short routes. At the **Left End** is an obvious **Buttress** split by two prominent cracks. In the middle is **Central Buttress** which has several fierce cracks of over 100 ft. (mostly unclimbed). Right of it is a prominent roof-capped corner – see routes below.

Calder Chimney. 110 ft. V. Diff. I. Clough, J. Greenwood. 21.5.67. The Left End Buttress. The left crack. Arrow at start. Climb chimney to ledge on right then traverse left across chimney to climb the left arête to big blocks and belay, 60 ft. Follow chimney to top.

Valhalla. 70 ft. Very Severe. N. Hill, D. Brown, C. Matthews. 21.3.75. Follows the steep crack immediately round the arête to the left of Calder Chimney. Traverse left at the edge at 30 ft. and finish up cracks above.

Fylde Crack. 130 ft. V. Diff. I. and N. Clough. 23.5.67. Start at arrow right of right crack. Climb up, then left by a narrow, slanting crack to join main chimney. From top of chimney climb slab on right.

Striding Edge. 100 ft. V. Diff. I. Clough, J. Greenwood. 23.5.67. Start, arrow, 20 yds. right of Fylde Crack. Climb slabby arête and cracked wall above to ledge, belay, 60 ft. Up overhanging crack an awkward groove above.

Grunt. 40 ft. Severe. I. Clough. 23.5.67. The slanting crack up th smooth wall just right of Striding Edge.

CENTRAL BUTTRESS AREA

Tyke Arête. 70 ft. V. Diff. I. Clough. 25.5.67. The arête left of th roof corner.

Layback Crack. 60 ft. Severe. I. Clough. 25.5.67. A prominent crac in the middle of a shallow bay right of the roof corner.

Trundle. 60 ft. Severe. N. Hill, D. Brown, C. Matthews. 21.3.7! Climb the corner just left of Layback Crack.

Grease Crack. 70 ft. V. Diff. I. Clough, J. Greenwood. 23.5.67. crack/chimney a few yards right of Layback Crack.

On the left end of the main face of Central Buttress, well left of th above routes, is an arête on which the following routes have bee recorded by N. Hill and D. Brown, 20.3.75.

Skrymir. 110 ft. Severe. Start on the arête, up to a prominen left-slanting crack which is followed to a ledge, 60 ft. On the wa above are two cracks. Take the left crack, 50 ft.

Asgard. 70 ft. Severe. The obvious groove right of the arête.

The Pink. 100 ft. Very Severe. Take the second corner to the right (Asgard, just right of the highest part of the face. Up jamming crack t ledge then follow right hand corner cracks to top.

ASKIVAL WEST RIDGE

From the Bealach an Oir. An easy ridge with some scrambling at th top which can be turned on the south.

NORTH WEST FACE

This impressive face can be seen from Barkeval, Hallival, (Trollaval. It rises from steep and broken slopes, so gives fir situations on excellent rock, routes up to 350 ft. **Approach:** Fro

Kinloch, to Bealach Barkeval and across the Atlantic Corrie to the Bealach an Oir, up the West Ridge to easy rake across under the crags. Allow 2 hrs. The ground below the crags is steep, loose and broken and a high level traverse in from the north is not really possible: which has left an area, the west flank of the North Ridge and a big recess (amphitheatre) as virgin territory. The North West Face is to the right of this. Despite several parties' work it is impossible to completely clarify descriptions here. Some are left out, including shorter routes and the first climb in the 20's by Botterill, O'Brien and Wells. Included is Atlantic Ridge; searching for this is a Rhum game in which all may play; it, however, rendered confusion complete as subsequent routes were linked to a variety of "Atlantic Ridges".

The face breaks up into a number of prominent ribs and ridges, the two major to the left, with the fine Askival Slab. Then there is No. 1 Gully, One-Two Buttress, No. 2 Gully and easier ground towards the N. Ridge.

Edinburgh Climb. 350 ft. Severe. I. Smart, H. Nichol, M. Slesser. 1.8.47. Lies on the part of the face looking almost north which can be seen from the North Ridge. Cairn at start: an obvious defect in sheer cliffs. Easy rock for 15 ft. then groove, crux, traverse to shelf and belay, then line of least resistance to top rocks which are Diff. Fine route. No escape possible.

Askival Slab. 200 ft. Climbed by O.U.M.C. Party in June 1935. **Left Hand Edge.** V. Diff. **Right Hand Corner.** Severe.

Rolling-Pin Route. 200 ft. V. Diff. A. Waites-Fairbairn, E. Wrangham. 28.6.51. Start in gully 25 ft. right of Askival Slab. Gully broken at 80 ft. by overhang, then becomes a chimney. Go about 60 ft. up gully and out to belay on left. From here a slab, often wet, is climbed straight up to overhang. Up and right, crux, to corner. Traverse 6 ft. right and up to niche. Exit right, difficult, to easy traverse to chimney which is then climbed. Narrow exit. Easy 30 ft. to edge, cairn.

No. 1 Gully. About 30 yds. from previous route a trap gully with one or two pitches, if taken direct, one Diff. chockstone. Escapes always available.

One-Two Buttress. Really the third, southmost, of the ribs of this face, it has only a few moderate pitches.

Shearwater Rib. 190 ft. V. Diff. C. Jorgensen, H. and D Stembridge. 14.6.57. Ten yards left of One-Two Buttress a sound rib protrudes. Climb 40 ft. to a platform, sling belay. Swing from hold right and up nose to a large platform at about 85 ft. Continue above or detour by right, 35 ft. and finish by the east top section of 1-2 Buttress.

No. 2 Gully is a wide, rotten gully with no real climbing though the rocks beyond it to the south give good scrambling.

Atlantic Ridge. 350 ft. V. Diff. W. Murray, M. Ward. May '48. When the N.W. Face is seen from Trollaval, two long ridges stand out clearly. The right hand rib is the route. Start a few feet to right of sharp left-hand edge. Cairn. By way of a shallow crack 90 ft. to a platform on the edge. (Round left corner a deep, demarcating groove.) Continue a few yards to right up a very steep wall of 50 ft. Thereafter route goes all the way to the top, ending suddenly at the summit.

Atlantic Slab. 350 ft. V. Diff. S. R. Bateson, T. Little. 8.4.74. Seen from Atlantic Corrie there is a prominent slab running from the foot of the crag to finish slightly left of Askival's summit. The route follows this slab, starting just right of a large overhang about 100 yds left of the start of Altantic Ridge. Climb a crack to stance at 60 ft. and on up crack system to a slab (small arête to its right), 120 ft. Climb the slab, 60 ft. to a bay. The wall leading to the big slab above is climbed by a deep crack (large chokestone) and the slab followed to the top 110 ft.

TROLLAVAL, c.2300 ft.

The most central of the Cuillins and possibly the finest viewpoint owing something in fact to its smaller scale which sets off the larger peaks without losing the wide views to mainland, Skye and the Outer Hebrides. It also has the largest cliff on the island on which there is room for further serious routes.

Like Barkeval across the Atlantic Corrie (the upper cirque of Glen Harris) it runs east-west, where Allival-Askival and Ainshval-Gillian are orientated north-south. It has a twin topped summit, the west being slightly higher and though there is this airy summit ridge

The summit of Trollaval with Eigg beyond.   Photo by Donald J.Bennet

requiring care there is no real climbing on the flanks. The northern slopes are nowhere near as craggy as the O.S. map implies, though there are places here and low down on the north west above the Abhainn a' Ghlinne which might be worth investigation. Otherwise all the climbing is situated on the south side, below the West Ridge. The northern flank of Ainshval gives a good viewpoint.

Approaches from either Bealach an Oir or Bealach an Fhuarsin lead to summit with only optional scrambling and the airy summit ridge. The West Ridge from Harris is straightforward. The crags have to be reached over these cols or by taking the Harris road and following down the Long Loch fault to cross Glen Harris. The corrie to the west, Fiachanis, is known as The Sandy Corrie. Allow 2½ hrs. Kinloch to foot of climbs.

SUMMIT BUTTRESS
The obvious flank under the E. Summit. Too broken – or too overhanging to have yielded many routes.

Malindarra. 195 ft. Diff. G E. Little. 30.6.84. This route takes a line of short corners on the wall/buttress flanking the south side of

Trallaval's west peak, directly below the summit. Start in a grassy bay to the left of the gully descending from between Trallaval's twin peaks. A prominent band of lighter rock skirts the base of the wall. Climb corner system, without deviation, to the summit.

TRIANGULAR BUTTRESS

The West Ridge runs out for about a third of a mile before sloping off down towards Harris. This buttress can be seen from the summit tucked in under the south flank at the end of this levelish section of ridge. It is best seen from Ainshval, or near the big Harris Buttress. It stands out in obvious triangular shape. Main features are a central gully, wet and broken and to the right a high-angled slab, 100 ft. high and 150 ft. across. A short way to the west a slanting slab of 120 ft. gives an easy line of descent.

Ptarmigan Crack. 150 ft. Diff. J. Parish, G. Dutton, I. Smart. 6.8.47. Follows the chimney forming the right side of the triangle. Starts to left of its foot and leads to a prominent window and through a very small manhole. Grooves to right lead into the chimney and a variety of finishes.

Evasion. c. 150 ft. Severe. H. Nichol, M. Slesser. Starts 80 ft. to the left of Ptarmigan and goes up to a platform level with the foot of the chimney. A fine airy traverse to the right leads across into the chimney; above the manhole.

Botany Crack. 130 ft. Severe. D. Stewart, D. Bennet. 20.7.50. Starts, cairn, in a rectangular recess guarded by a fine 20 ft. pinnacle at the foot of the slab. Up the recess to a good platform, move a few feet left, and follow crack to the top.

Zigzag Route. 110 ft. Severe. A few yards right of Botany rises a peculiar serpentine crack. Climb this, then up left to a belay, then up right to a conspicuous overhung recess. The movement past the overhang is very difficult.

The Wandering Botanist. 120 ft. Hard Severe. D. Bearhop and A. Tibbs. 25.3.82. Climb zigzag to the recess then step left onto a wall and climb it till an overhang is reached. Traverse left under the overhang and finish up a crack which is the finish of Botany Crack.

Bloodstone Crack. 100 ft. Very Severe. M. Ward, W. Murray. May '48. To the left of the central gully is a steep, short crack. Cairn. The first pitch of 50 ft. is V.S. The start is strenuous and goes by the right wall. At 15 ft. the holds become tiny. Good stance above.

HARRIS BUTTRESS

Previous names have been dropped. This is not really a buttress but an impressive wall of gabbro across the south flank of Trollaval, some few hundred yards out from and down a bit from the Bealach an Fhuarain. It is 400 ft. high and several hundred yards wide, streaked in many colours. Its repulsive character hides some of the finest and longest climbing to be had on Rhum. The east end is rather wet. Best seen coming up from the Sandy Corrie by keeping over on the Ainshval side.

Guiding features: At centre of the buttress there is a not very definite rib, below which is a rock poised like a capstan. Shallow gullies run up on either side of the rib, each with a large overhang. About forty feet right of the right gully there is a vertical 250 ft. crack.

Guillotine. 410 ft. Very Severe. R. Barton, D. Morris. June '79. This follows the 250 ft. crack mentioned above which, in its upper reaches, becomes twin parallel grooves. A good, sustained climb.

Climb the crack and move right to a good ledge below the right-hand groove (40 ft., 12m). Climb up to the bulge guarding the right-hand groove, avoid this by following the left-hand groove a short distance, when a delicate traverse leads back into the original groove and a ledge on its right (50 ft., 15m). Move left to a small pinnacle perched between the grooves. Climb into the bay above, escape by a steep crack on the left and move left to a large block ledge (80 ft., 24m). Move back right under the Guillotine and use it to surmount the short, steep corner. Follow pleasant ramps and grooves to belay below a large white slab (120 ft., 36m). The slab now leads easily to a junction with Archangel. Escape is also possible leftwards (120 ft., 36m).

Archangel Route. 400 ft. V. Diff. M. Ward, W. Murray. May '48. About forty feet right of the 250 ft. crack, see above, a shallow and broken depression runs up the rocks. 60 ft. up at top left of the depression a block pinnacle, the base dangerously shattered looking, so climb the rocks to the left of the depression to a platform left of the pinnacle. Scramble over the pinnacle, "spread wings of faith, and take a short, bold flight across the gap to a chimney on the right-hand side of the depression". Chimney becomes a vertical 20 ft. crack, good holds. Follow a broad ledge right, turn a corner into a small bay under a great groove. 20 ft. up the groove climb up left to narrow ridge. Follow this until it falls back among broad slabs which steepen into the line of overhangs crossing the buttress. Climb diagonally up left towards a steep corner where a delightful, exposed climb is had on a rough gabbro slab, the last difficulty. A route of interest and character.

Archangel, Variation Start. V. Diff. A. Waites-Fairbairn, E. Wrangham. 2.7.51. Start 40 ft., right, of Archangel. Steep rocks lead up a sort of groove. The route then trending right and up for 150 ft. to the foot of 'the great groove'. (Small cairn at start.)

Central Rib. 300 ft. Hard Severe. D. Stewart, D. Bennet. 22.7.50. Start at the lowest point of the rocks, a few yards above the capstan. Cairn. After the initial overhang, a groove and easier slabs lead to the foot of the rib where it becomes a definite and almost vertical arête. Climb the crest, or just to the right of it, for two pitches, to a small, finely placed platform. Cairn. Two further pitches up slabs and steep corners to finish on sloping grass terrace. Cairn. Upper slopes of mountain can be reached by short wall directly above, or by easier slabs to right. One of the best routes on Rhum.

Right Central Gully. 300 ft. V. Diff. Waites-Fairbairn, E. Wrangham. 2.7.51. The straight black gully slanting right; just right of Central Rib. Start as for Central Rib but where it steepens go right over easy ground to the foot of the gully. Awkward to start and two further pitches lead to a belay, below where the gully divides into two chimneys. (Right one, severe.) Ahead a steep crack with useful flake on right wall. Follow various cracks for over 100 ft. to a chimney with a prominent chockstone and the finish.

Harris Sweater. 300 ft. VS 4c. J. Fotheringham, R. Allan. 1.5.83. The obvious crack and groove line 20 ft. right of the black central corner. Fine climbing to below the hanging flake (mentioned by Barton on Guillotine). 1. Straight up the crack, belay below 20 ft. overhanging crack/corner, 150 ft. 2. Up the overhanging crack, up the corner by the Guillotine, flake and ramps to Archangel, 150 ft.

Harris Tweed. 450 ft. VS. J. Fotheringham, R. Allan. 1.5.83. This climbs the obvious corner which Archangel avoids. (Some easy ground.) 1. Straight up the corner, moving right at the top, 150 ft. 2. Follow the rightward fault, 150 ft. 3. Break up through the rough slabs for a steep corner line at the right hand end of the upper buttress, 150 ft.

Black Day. 400 ft. VS. J. Fotheringham, R. Allan. 1.5.83. (This may be a variation of Guillotine.) The black central corner was climbed to the top section, whence an escape traverse was made right to eventually join Archangel. There was a hard section at 80 ft., moving right to avoid a steep, loose section.

Hagar. 100 ft. HVS. A. Kirk, A. Lumsden. 2.6.86. The climb starts at a small cairn 30m from the west end of the cliff. Climb thin crack, move into obvious niche (crux), and up this to the top.

Lucky Eddy. 100 ft. VS. G. Swinton, J. Mitchell. 2.6.86. Start 10m left of Hagar at obvious left-facing corner. Climb crack to ledge below steep corner which is climbed direct or by the arête to the right. Finish up right.

RUINSIVAL, 1607 ft.
This peak with its low-lying north west facing crags has had a proliferation of routes, often badly described; so without shedding tears, shorter/easier routes have been left out and text and diagrams made to agree. (S.M.C. Guide to the Islands, 1971, is particularly bad on Ruinsival.)

Ruinsival is best climbed from a base on Harris Bay. Camps should keep away from cows. Driftwood in plenty. The crags are a long way from Kinloch or Dibidil bothy; from the former use the Harris road or cut through the Long Loch fault, or come over the Bealach Barkeval; from the latter cross the Bealach an Fhuarain, along the Leac a' Chaisteil or round the south west coast. The crags are often clear in bad westerly weather when higher crags are ruled out. The long Leac fails to match the O.S. map's impressive delineation. The Rangail River is bridged ¼ mile up from the shore. Forty minutes from Harris. The crags are described as follows.

LOWER TIER
About 100 yards below and right of Giant's Staircase there is a long chunky line of buttresses forming the Lower Tier. They have been named:–

RUINSIVAL North West Crags

HB Highlander's Buttress
GW Green Wall
FF Fiachanis Face
XX Giant's Staircase

to Loch Fiachanis

1. **North Buttress.** 2. **Woden's Wall** (behind/right of N.B.). 3. **Thor's Buttress.** 4. **Frigga's Buttress** (across a break). 5. **South Buttress.**

MIDDLE TIER

Two areas. 1. Above 2-5 of Lower Tier lies the unmistakable **Highlander's Buttress** with a bare wall on its left and a series of grooves and arêtes on its right. 2. Across from this, right (west), beyond the wide stone shoot is a considerable area of rock, distinguished by the big green platforms in the centre; this is the **Green Wall.** Its climbs are partly spoiled by several horizontal ledges.

SUMMIT TIER

The crags above, left of Green Wall, overlooking the big stone shoot.

Giant's Staircase. A series of nine rock steps forming a long ridge to the left of the above Tiers. Described below.

Fiachanis Face. Lies east of the Giant's Staircase and is a two-tiered corrie almost, which is largely unclimbed. See below. It lies immediately south and above L. Fiachanis. Left of this again is a big prow and various crags, all unexplored. Climb up from east side of the loch.

LOWER TIER: 1. NORTH BUTTRESS

North Corner. 120 ft. Mod. Up a Chimney just right of the north corner.

Riona. 120 ft. Severe. A. Littlejohn. 10.7.59. 100 ft. right of N. Corner, a 40 ft. triangular flake, deep damp gully to left, wet overhang high right. From cairn up the most prominent part of flake to stance at 40 ft. Move left, swing round by a perched block to large ledge, possibly unsound. Up steep wall above slightly right, finishing directly above the start.

Slab and Groove. 150 ft. V. Diff. J.M.C.Y. 1945-46. Few yards left of centre of buttress an obvious break in rock wall, where a slab is followed right, then awkward groove left to a triangular grass ledge, exit by slab on right, or (harder) straight up.

Cracked Rib. 150 ft. Very Severe. D. Stewart, D. Bennet, S. Paterson. 18.7.50. A few yards left of Demolition Crack is a rib with an overhanging base, split by a vertical crack. Cairn. Up 60 ft. past a heather shelf to recess under and just right of the rib, spike belay. Traverse to rib and follow it on right for 40 ft. to shelf, belay. Final 15 ft. climb on left of rib.

Perdita's Traverse. 140 ft. V. Diff. A. Littlejohn, A. Clark. 5.7.59. Left of the start of Slab and Groove is an arête and then two grooves. Climb the left groove to broad ledge, 40 ft. From its right end down round an airy corner and right into the right-hand groove. Take, crux, the projecting staircase on the right side of this groove to a large stance on arête. Finish up right side of arête.

Demolition Crack. 120 ft. Severe. H. Nichol, I. Smart, M. Slesser. 5.8.47. To the left of the south corner of the buttress is a deep groove which cuts the face, V-shaped in lower part. A subsidiary groove, 20 ft. left, is taken to a flake at 50 ft. Traverse right to enter corner in main groove and ascend directly. The direct ascent of the main groove, 60 ft., V. Diff. was climbed in 1950 by Stewart, Bennet, Paterson.

South Corner. 100 ft. Mod. Up just right of the corner.

LOWER TIER: 2 WODEN'S WALL

Sloping Ledge. 85 ft. V. Diff. Consensus from vague accounts: Starts directly above Demolition Crack cairn. Ascend to sloping ledge beneath a large funnel of slabs and enter funnel at end of ledge, probably severe, or continue to right over a groove and then up.

Airy Mary. 120 ft. V. Diff. H. Nichol, G. Dutton. 9.8.47. Cairn at start. Up corner crack 40 ft. left of rib on left of Bill's. Very steeply thereafter, then eases, loose. Finish by slab and rib to left.

Sentry's Sortie. 100 ft. V. Diff. A. Littlejohn, A. Clark. 10.7.59. Between the central break in the face and the south corner there is a large shattered arête. 15 ft. left, cairn, take a steep 20 ft. crack over two ledges to the crest of the arête, which is followed a few feet to grassy platform block belay. Cross the groove to the right and climb up 15 ft., enter sentry box to right and exit by corner above it, crux.

Bill's. 100 ft. Diff. J.M.C.Y. 1945-46. Goes up the much-broken slab to the right of the central break.

Woden's Walk. 120 ft. V. Diff. I. Smart, H. Nichol, M. Slesser. 5.8.47. Ascend obvious crack on right of Bill's. After first pitch 90 ft. traverse right to near top of Peretz. Runner possible. Exposed.

Woden's Crack. 120 ft. V. Diff. D. Stewart, D. Bennet, S. Paterson. 18.7.50. Start as for the Walk but climb straight up the crack where the Walk goes right.

Peretz Corner. 120 ft. Diff. J.M.C.Y. '45-'46. The big ridge to the right of the wall. Tower-like from below. Start round corner to right.

Groove and Chimney. 100 ft. Diff. A. Littlejohn, A. Clark. 10.7.59. Take groove right of shattered arête up to grass platform of Sentry's, and on 15 ft. as before, then traverse left over flake to ledge, whence short chimney up.

LOWER TIER: 3 THOR'S BUTTRESS

Chuckiestane Groove. 120 ft. Severe. A. Littlejohn, A. Dinwoodie. 23.6.61. Cairn at highest point of grass-scree between Woden's and Thor's, below wet groove between 2 overhangs. Climb left wall till forced into groove, last few feet of it the crux. Easier ground, good stance, 60 ft. Continue groove 20 ft., at easier angle and finish 20 ft. up steep wall.

Right Chimney. 120 ft. V. Diff. A. Littlejohn, A. Dinwoodie. 23.6.61. Far back on left flank of Thor's two obvious chimneys. (Right of Chuckiestane.) Take the narrow, steep right one throughout.

June Jigsaw. 80 ft. V. Diff. A. Littlejohn, A. Dinwoodie. 22.6.61. Right flank of Buttress, cairn at large dissected slab. Follow deep crack left, right by ledge to vertical crack, blocks, then easy to top.

LOWER TIER: 4 FRIGGA'S BUTTRESS

Gothic Crack. 70 ft. V. Diff. A. Littlejohn, A. Dinwoodie. 22.6.61. The wide crack edging the huge frontal flake of Frigga's. From top of arch on up centre to top.

Yellowstone Chimney. 80 ft. Diff. A. Littlejohn. 21.6.61. The chimney between buttresses 4 and 5. Yellow wall on left. Crux at top.

LOWER TIER: 5. SOUTH BUTTRESS

Curving Chimney. 90 ft. Diff. A. Littlejohn, A. Dinwoodie. 22.6.61. On right flank a deep, damp chimney curves up right and is climbed on left wall to chockstones and on to awkward exit.

South Crack. 65 ft. V. Diff. Beyond Curving Chimney, past grassy, overhung corner to first weakness: steep crack above big block, wall on right, steep nose.

MIDDLE TIER: 1. HIGHLANDER BUTTRESS

The Creep. The face on the left is bounded, left, by a slanting gully. This route cuts up across it. 50 ft. Diff. The rest of the wall is vertical and intimidating.

Seoras. 150 ft. Very Severe. J. Matyssek, H. Brown. 20.6.66. Towards the right of the face is a dark, triangular depression (seen from afar). Climb to the apex of the triangle and then over, crux above to a groove. (Ledge up from left to here is unclimbed.) Follow the groove (V. Diff.) and take right fork to end at cairn at top of No. 1 Arête. The first chink in the defences of a fine wall. Right of the face is the series of arêtes and grooves; these give peculiarly enjoyable climbing. No. 1 Arête is the one edging the face. No. 1 Groove is to its right, then No. 2 Arête and so on.

Fingerless. 130 ft. Very Severe. A. Nisbet, S. R. Bateson. 12.4.74. The prominent crack 40 ft. left of Seoras is climbed to a rightward-trending ledge which is followed to the base of a crack which is then climbed to the top.

No. 1 Arête. 170 ft. Mild Severe. J. Matyssek, H. Brown, J. Patterson, W. Simpson. 20.6.66. Start at lowest point and scramble to steepening, belay. Overhang, crux, onto surprising pedestal and then final grooves. Cairn at top.

Hallelujah Heave-Up. 180 ft. Severe. I. Smart, M. Slesser, H. Nichol, G. Dutton. 5.8.47. In No. 2 Groove. Difficult rocks lead to a wall ascended at corner by loose block. From large shelf traverse right onto left wall of No. 3 Arête for 10 ft., then ascend crux groove. Traverse left round corner and up slab to heave-up.

Jawbone Crack. 125 ft. Hard Severe. H. Nichol, G. Dutton. 9.8.47.

Up No. 3 Groove till forced by overhang onto right wall, crux. Delicate move to re-enter Groove above.

Bachelor's Choice. 160 ft. V. Diff. H. Nichol, J. Parish. 8.8.47. First 2 pitches of Hallelujah, 60 ft. then traverse left to No. 2 Arête round a sensational corner to a prominent ledge. Then an 80 ft. traverse across vertical wall astride a long flake to top of No. 1 Groove. Exposed.

Variant. A. Littlejohn, A. Clark. 6.7.59. As above to round sensational corner to No. 2 Arête. Follow it for 15 ft., then traverse left along exposed ledge for 25 ft. and descend slightly, with difficulty, to belay in the corner. Climb corner for 10 ft. and continue traverse left to exposed corner, descend 10 ft. to broad exposed ledge which is followed for 20 ft. to a long, narrow slab forming its continuation 25 ft. up it to top.

MIDDLE TIER: 2 GREEN WALL

Campion Slab. The left side of Green Wall has a rough, steep set, diamond-shaped slab. This is Campion Slab. It gives V. Diff. climbing up to 60 ft. by the curving crack, or up from the flake to the right. H. Brown, J. Matyssek and party. 20.6.66.

Face Route. 200 ft. Severe. J. Matyssek, T. Izatt, S. Crockatt. 20.6.66. The cairned start lies 25 ft. left of the rake running up to the Green Platforms, at the foot of a trap dyke. Climb up left by crack to ledge and follow cracks straight up the wall over two further ledges and finish up a wide 50 ft. crack. Cairn at top.

Very Well. 100 ft. V. Diff. M. H. Moar, J. D. Roberts-James. June '70. The climb follows the rib bounding the right side of the gully/chimney right of Face Route.

Claymore. 260 ft. Very Severe. J. Matyssek, H. Brown. 24.5.67. Start, cairn, 15 ft. right of Face Route. Along right on trap dyke for 12 ft. to small platform. Break up strenuously by crack on face left to perched block on a terrace. Cairn. Continuing cracks on wall, 80 ft. Cairn. Easier 50 ft. wall to larger terrace where escape possible but best finish up crack on nose, cairn at foot, for 80 ft. More strenuous than attractive as a route.

Right Corner. 150 ft. V. Diff. J. Matyssek, H. Brown, S. Menmuir 20.6.66. The far right of Green Wall has a tongue of slab with an undercut crack to the right. Climb up beside this crack on the slabs o corner. Difficulties in top section.

Right Corner Chimney. 130 ft. Diff. H. Brown, W. Simpson, J. Yule 20.6.66. The tongue of slabs is bound on the left by this chimney

SUMMIT TIER

Shearwater Chimney. 170 ft. V. Diff. J. Parish, H. Nichol. 8.8.47. Above and to the left of the face of the buttress, the chimney rise steeply out of a wide gully, the upper section being overhanging Chockstone belay at 120 ft., then finish over hanging block and through chockstone window above.

Shearwater Arête. 150 ft. Diff. J. G. Parish, H. Nichol. 8.8.47. The arête to left of the chimney, from its top move to the right up a vertical wall.

Avalanche Avenue. 70 ft. Severe. J. Parish, H. Nichol, 8.8.47. On a small buttress left and up the stone shoot from the above. Ascend prominent groove, traverse left to terrace and up a rather loose funnel above.

The Whited Crack. 110 ft. V. Diff. C. G. M. Slesser, I. H. M. Smart 9.8.47. The obvious white crack in the peridotite wall of the gully above Shearwater Arête. often greasy.

Giant's Staircase. c. 600 ft. V. Diff. (Severe variant pitch). J. G Parish, H. Nichol. 8.8.47. This series of nine rock steps gives a good climb. The second, fourth and fifth steps are V. Diff.; Mod.-Diff thereafter. Against the fifth step is a pinnacle which can be seen from afar. It is Severe by the face. An unpleasant step off it onto a steep 20 ft. wall follows. The ridge ends near the summit plateau.

FIACHANIS FACE

Bulging Wall. The name given to an intimidating unclimbed wall we across the top tier going east. An overhanging recess on its left migh be climbable.

Fork Slab. Fifty yards east of Bulging Wall is an 80 ft. spikey wall a an easier angle. In its centre a crack forks at 15 ft. into three prong-like cracks. These were all climbed, 20.6.66. V. Diff. H. Brown, J. Matyssek, and party.

AINSHVAL, 2552 ft. to SGURR NAN GILLEAN, 2503 ft.

These are no longer peaks of the good basic rocks, but quartz felsite and other igneous variants, which can be greasy and friable in places. The traverse of this group completes the full traverse of the Rhum Cuillins, so is described from north to south.

AINSHVAL, 2552 ft.

NORTH RIDGE

Above the Bealach an Fhuarain, 1730 ft., is a steepish buttress starting this ridge; it can be climbed or turned on the west. Beyond the levelling-off above the ridge again steepens; either scramble or turn on the east this time, where there is a scree-filled corrie, the **Grey Corrie**. The summit, second highest in Rhum, lies round the Grey Corrie rim a bit where the East Ridge joins the main ridge. In Jan. '46, E. Peretz and I. Smart found the North Ridge to be V. Diff. under winter conditions.

MUNRO'S RIDGE

From the Bealach an Fhuarain traverse the northern flank screes to gain the definite crest further west. There is a jammed block at one stage forming a window. (The northern flank rocks, above the screes, are very friable.) This is presumably the ridge Munro took in 1891, flattering it with "a nice bit of real rock climbing with some rather awkward smooth slabs".

EAST RIDGE

At the foot of this ridge, above Glen Dibidil, starting at the 1000 ft. level is a buttress of 'Douglas Boulder' appearance on a small scale. This gave a 250 ft. Mod. line (J. Parish 1947) left of parallel grass gullies; there is a wide variety of choice, possibly harder to the left. The long ridge above gives good scrambling. Heading for Kinloch it has been descended as a short cut to the Bealach an Oir.

The O.S. map delineates the eastern flanks of these peaks badly. From the summit of Ainshval follow the rim of a second corrie, the **Forgotten Corrie**, to an unimpressive subsidiary summit, a mere rise, **Sgurr nan Goibhrean**, 2475 ft., not named on map. It has an easy East

Sgurr nan Gillean - Ainshval
seen over the Bealach an Oir - Trallval ridge (taken from Barkeval)

Ridge to Glen Dibidil (of which there is no note of an ascent), and to the long Leach a' Chaisteal branching west and then slightly north of west to Ruinsival.

SGURR NAN GILLEAN, 2503 ft.

Between Goibhrean and Gillean lies a third corrie, locally called the **Nameless Corrie**. It has easy-angled slabs in its lower reaches and high up, just under the summit of Gillean, is a steep cliff of 200-300 ft.: nasty-looking and unclimbed, though often remarked on.

Sgurr nan Gillean is the southmost peak and a fine viewpoint. Descent to Dibidil is not entirely straightforward as the top section is steep, broken ground while below lies a steep grass flank, which "merits V.S. grading at the end of a long day". It is best to aim a bit to the south and flank down thereafter. There is nothing of interest on the long slopes between Gillean and Ruinsival on the south west.

CLIMBS IN OTHER AREAS

PINNACLES AND STACKS

Nowhere big but always amusing; many will prove awkward to approach.

Stac nam Faoileann. About a mile before Dibidil coming from Kinloch. On map. Climbed in May 1967 by I. Clough and party by a groove on the landward side, possibly the easiest way. 40 ft. Diff.

Stac nam Faoileann II. A little to the south of the above and more shapely. Diff., climbed after descending the sea cliffs for 100 ft.

STAC NAM FAOILEANN CLIFFS

Tidal Exit Cracks. 80 ft. MVS. K. Connor, D. Bannerman, A. Rendal. April 1983. Start in recess directly opposite the rear of the stack and climb corner to exit round overhang onto ledge, then left and up diagonal cracks (steep) to small niche, 15 ft. below top. Climb (crux) on small holds up niche and mantleshelf.

Big Boots & Trainers. 80 ft. HVS. K. Connor, D. Bannerman. April 1983. The deep-cut chimney at the landward N. side of the point. Abseil down to flat rocks at base of chimney. Up chimney to sloping ledge on left. Climb left crack to reach a bulge, which is surmounted, then continue up centre of chimney to final mantleshelf.

STOATIR POINT

This is the obvious point c 20 mins from Dibidil on the path to Kinloch. The following are on the light-coloured South Face of the cliff. Abseil from block to reach starts.

Iso-Amylase. 70 ft. Severe. W. Wright, J. Rose. 25.3.80. Abseil to large shelf by big crack trending left. Climb the crack to shelf, walk right to corner and climb it, step right and finish right of abseil bollard.

The Rozzer. 90 ft. VS. J. Rose, W. Wright. 25.3.80. Abseil as above and traverse just above sea-level to obvious niche at edge of crag. Step left onto slab arête, climb corner and awkward bulge. Traverse 6 ft. right on large shelf then climb up leftwards (crack) to finish on thin holds.

Ocean of Mercy. 75 ft. VS. W. Wright, G. Eadie. 28.3.80. Start as for Iso. Go directly up wall slightly left to crack for small chock at 15 ft. Right on small holds to corner with sloping shelves. Move up to large ledge and belay. Move left along ledge and finish up Iso.

Morning Tide. 90 ft. VS. W. Wright, G. Eadie. 28.3.80. Start 10 ft. left and a bit lower than for Iso. Move up 4 ft. then traverse left on

The Papadil Stack

small holds across wall. Up to small ledge then traverse to top of Rozzer corner. Mantleshelf as for Rozzer then move right and up wall to ledge. Left along it to obvious flake. Climb this and finish on loose blocks left of Rozzer.

The obvious stack off this point was climbed by Wright and Eadie, 28.3.80. After abseiling as above they traversed right and through a tunnel to the N. side from which the stack is accessible at low tide. A ramp led to the seaward side and the top. It proved only Diff.

Dibidil shore is slotted with some impressive "zawns" and there is plenty of scrambling hereabouts with some chances for serious climbs.

Papadil Pinnacle. About 30 ft. At the seaward end of the loch. Easiest line is a scramble.

Fist and Finger Stack. South east of Sgor an t-Snide (two miles south of Harris), a striking double stack joined by a neck to the shore and needing low tide approach. H. Brown and N. Hunter, 1.6.70. V. Diff. Cross to the south end of the stack and up to a pedestal. Follow weaknesses left, then right to final wall and overhang. Take the curving "Pinkey Crack" up left. (The Finger at the far end is unreached.)

Sgor an t-Snide. On the main point between Papdil and Harris, a small stack visible from Harris. Low tide needed to make the seaward side (by a southern detour) whence scramble up to a sneck at the north end then onto the "Sea Roofs": two steep slabs, the first crossed to its top right to gain the upper to the summit – where the Guillemots nest. Very Diff. H. Brown. 1.6.70.

Harris also has a small pinnacle in the bay, climbed long ago, and several slots and walls. Just north of Harris, the bay walls are sheer and higher and would give some climbing if allowed.

North Side. There is little climbing here as the sandstone offers little scope. Any visits to this part of the island must be arranged with the Chief Warden first. In the interests of the wildlife climbing is not really encouraged on these hills or on sea cliffs.

It must be borne in mind that Rhum is a Nature Reserve and one of its interests is the seabird life and the cliff nests. These should not be disturbed and ANYWHERE ON THE ISLAND, "gardening" should be kept to the minimum.

One report of exploration in the NW says the rock was generally rather loose and vegetated but the big "sail" of rock at Schooner Point "is an unrelenting array of shattered pillars, all overlapping the wrong way".

Orval has an interesting 100 ft. pinnacle at the foot of its northern cliffs. This has been variously described as "sensational" or "hopelessly loose" so has naturally proved irresistible.

In 1977 Hamish MacInnes and Dave Bathgate reached the top by somewhat unconventional methods: they abseiled down the Orval cliff face, lassoed the top and then crossed on the tensioned rope. During this escapade Orval threw a boulder down, injuring Ian Nicholson. He received medical treatment from the island's vets. The team reckoned a conventional ascent would be highly dangerous.

The first conventional ascent was made by G. E. Little on 18.7.85 (see SMCJ 1986, p164). Much loose rock was thrown down but the Pinnacle still survives, as does Mr Little. 100 ft. XS 5b E3.

Start at a slight groove on the right hand side of the pinnacle, just down from the 'neck'. Climb the groove (4a) to a small ledge on the outward face of the pinnacle. Climb the face, with a move left to gain another small ledge (5b). Continue up the face, with a move onto the left edge, to gain the small flat topped summit (5b).

BEINN NAN STAC

Wet Crack. J. Orr, P. Bloomfield. Seen from the bothy there are three areas of tumbled rocks below the lowest, nearest line of cliff. The above is hidden in above the top right corner of the middle lot. There is a deep cut chimney with chockstones. Go through under these and climb the 50 ft. dripping chimney at the back of the chasm. (The left outer edge of this deep cut chimney would make a good route – Ed.)

Brown Trousers. I. Swann. 180 ft. VS. This tackles the slab right of the above which lead one to the obvious grassy corner. The crux is the exit from this along a wide sloping ledge, exposed, until hands can reach holds above. Pull round the corner and up onto grass.

This area would repay further exploration. Much of the Stac crags are disappointingly over-steep or sopping. There is a hard-looking crack line right of the huge cave in the main crag area and the best of

Dave Bathgate and Hamish MacInnes on top of the Orval Pinnacle

the rock at the uphill end might offer a route as could the walls of the well-hidden hollow below the summit. The left skyline, seen from Dibidil, was climbed while looking at these crags.

Ankle. H. M. Brown. 8.7.86. V. Diff. Follows the last of the rocks on the flank of Beinn nan Stac. Cairn. A slab left of a hanging V of rock leads one left to the edge, then break back and up steeply to a bouldery ledge and grass terrace, 80 ft. Easy ground thereafter, with odd scrambles, up ridge to top of the hill.

Walkers approaching Beinn Nan Stac from the Askival can turn the barring rock wall to the left (north).

CLIMBS ON THE ISLAND OF EIGG

The following climbs have been listed here for convenience. By careful study of steamer timetables, it is possible to fit in a day or two on Eigg going to and from Rhum. These notes are virtually those of the late Ian Clough; sadly missed in the islands as elsewhere. For general information on accommodation, sailings, and so on see *A Guide to Eigg and Muck* or contact Mr Lawrence MacEwan, Isle of Muck, by Mallaig, Inverness-shire (0687-2362) or The Estate Office, Island of Eigg, by Mallaig, Inverness-shire (0687-82413). Both islands have shops and either self-catering or guest house accommodation and campers are welcomed. Muck has limited climbing but is green and pleasant. Eigg has plenty of scope, both on the Sgurr and elsewhere. Wildlife should be disturbed as little as possible. Canna (National Trust for Scotland) has cliffs which may repay investigation – no reports. Contact the NTS representative, Canna, by Mallaig, Inverness-shire (0687-2466).

An Sgurr (or Scuir, etc.) is the highest point on the island and makes it a prominent landmark from afar, for it rises from its encircling cliffs to a prow in the east which is unique; the overhanging nose is about 400 ft. high. Walkers can climb the Sgurr without difficulty. Go west from Galmisdale House along the northern side until the cliffs turn to scree. Once on the ridge, go along to the east end: a fine situation as can be imagined.

NORTH FACE OF AN SGURR
There are some attractive possibilities. 200 yards west of the Nose where there is a moderate zig-zag route (not recommended in wet weather).

The Sgurr of Eigg

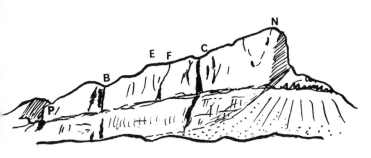

AN SGURR South Face

B   Botterill's Crack
F   The Flue
N   The Nose
E   Eagle Chimney
C   Collie's Cleft
P   Purphura

SOUTH FACE OF AN SGURR

This wall is of columnar pitchstone porphyry and is about a mile long. In the west only is it broken by easy grassy gullies. Between these gullies and the nose, this rampart is cut across by Long Ledge at a little less than half height and below the steepest part of the face. The upper wall is split into three sections by two deep recesses: Collie's Cleft, and further west, Botterill's Crack. The rock has proved sound on the chimney lines, but is possibly loose on open faces. A footnote in S.M.C. Journal, 1908, says Collie "climbed the rock a short distance west of the south side of extreme point".

Botterill's Crack. 170 ft. Severe. I. Clough, J. Davidson, C. Greatwich. 12.4.67. A heathery gully leads to a big bay at the level of Long Ledge. In the bay are 3 well defined chimneys and cracks; follow the left of these. (Some way up left wall are two chimney lines.) The climb was named after a pioneer here and in Rhum in 1922.

Eagle Chimney. 250 ft. Hard Severe. I. Clough, C. Greatwich. 14.4.67. Prominent and near the centre of this face (another chimney further right becomes prominent higher up, Eagle is more distinct in lower part). Approach as for Botterill's and walk along Long Ledge. The first 110 ft. pitch is continuously difficult.

The Flue. 270 ft. Very Severe. D. Nicol, P. Gunn. 18.6.67. This is the chimney right of Eagle, most distinct in upper half. Approach via Long Ledge, climb heathery rocks and gain base of chimney, 35 ft. Follow the shallow chimney, then a steep wall on the right to a restricted stance at the back of a second chimney, 70 ft. Up chimney to terrace, 80 ft., then trend left up pleasant slabs to top, 85 ft.

Collie's Cleft. 200 ft. Severe. I. Clough, C. Greatwich, 13.4.67. The large corner recess immediately west of the uncompromising columnar wall leading to the Nose. Approach by obvious heather gully, awkward entry. Take the deep chimney at the back of the corner to a ledge, belays, 80 ft. Continue up the vertical left chimney which has unpleasant exit, 120 ft.

The Nose. 300 ft. Very Severe and A.3. C. Boulton, K. Jones. 1970. Start at foot of steep, left-slanting groove, directly beneath the central overhanging section. Climb thin crack in steep wall past a small overhang, then past loose flakes to small stance, peg belay, 100 ft. 20 ft. right, along obvious ramp, until possible to peg up green flutes, trending slightly right (tied-off knife blades, 6 bolts) to gain stance, bolt belay on steep wall above overhang, 100 ft. Step left and climb straight up wall to top, 100 ft. (2 pegs).

Purphura. 400 ft. Very Severe. P. Moores, S. Whaley. 25.5.78. Near the left end of the face there is an easy, open gully, used in the descent. This route starts to the right of the gully, under a small roof, and follows an obvious, ramp/corner-like feature, trending rightwards up slatey rock.

Climb a groove to the small roof, exit right and climb slabs to reach a very obvious, horizontal fault belay (130 ft.). Move up and left across a smooth slab, then slightly down before breaking through the tiered overhangs. Follow slabs to the top (140 ft.). Easy climbing to finish (130 ft.).

Recent Routes

A great deal of excellent climbing (routes from V. Diff. to E4), mostly on the upper tier of the Sgurr, with the rock "better than gabbro", have been made in 1986, 1987 by Graham Little and friends. Full descriptions appear in the 1988 Scottish Mountaineering Club Journal.

NORTHERN EIGG

The northern half of the island is a moorland plateau which is virtually surrounded by cliffs of 100 to 500 ft. They are apt to be sadly broken by skirting grass terraces. Two most impressive sections, one on N. side, one on E., might repay investigation.

On the West Side, overlooking Cleadale and Laig Bay, are the following routes:

Cleadale Face. A tall pillar culminating in a crazy pillar is the most obvious feature. **Laig Buttress** is a clean flying buttress on the extreme right, a small Sphynx-like pinnacle to its right, a little rock amphitheatre behind.

Grit. 150 ft. Severe. I. Clough, C. Greatwich, J. Davidson, N. Clough. 11.4.67. From cairn climb a groove to ledge, 40 ft., peg belay. Up right into a corner, up into an overhanging niche on left and swing up left again to stance, 60 ft., peg belay. Continue to top.

The Pod. 150 ft. Very Severe. I. Clough, C. Greatwich. 11.4.67.

Climb the groove which culminates in a short overhanging corner crack, the crux. More easily to top.

Poll nam Partan Crags; just north of the Galmisdale pier in bay of Pall nam Partan are some steep, much cracked, gritstone-like crags of about 70 ft., which offer good sport.

NEW ROUTES

Send two copies of routes to Hamish Brown, 21 Carlin Craig, Kinghorn, Fife KY3 9RX – one will be forwarded to the current new routes editor of the Scottish Mountaineering Club Journal, the other filed for future guidebook revision.

Please write on one side of paper only, type if possible; proper names, if written, in BLOCK CAPITALS where first mentioned and do use names in keeping with the character of the island.

Bibliography

The following is a selection of titles of general and background interest or of specific reference to the Island of Rhum. Where books are out of print dates are given and these can be ordered from libraries. The Reserve Handbook has a very full bibliographical appendix. The office on Rhum has a range of current publications on sale and the Chief Warden can arrange for interested people to study their extensive collection of papers and files on any topic.

Aslet, C.:*Kinloch Castle, Isle of Rhum*. Country Life. 9 and 16 August 1984 (a good look at this showpiece mansion).

Banks, N.: *Six Inner Hebrides*. David & Charles 1977. (Useful summary of Rhum and Its Neighbours).

Best, A.*Return of the Sea Eagles*. The Field. 21.9.85.

Bourne, W. R. P.: *The Birds of the Island of Rhum*. Scot. Nat. vol. 69, 21-31.

Brown, H. M.: *A Week on Rhum*. Scotland's Mag. March 1973. : *Rum – Isle of Surprises*. Scots Mag. November 1966. : *The Secret Island of Rhum*. Countryman. Winter 1968.

Butterfield, I.: *Dibidil*. MBA 1971. (Story of bothy restoration).

Campbell, J. L.: *Canna*. (A thorough study).

Cameron, A.: *This Was My Rum*. Scots Mag. August 1979. (Bullough days reminiscences).

Chinery, M.: *A Field Guide to the Insects of Britain & Northern Europe*. Collins.

Clutton-Brock, T.: *The Red Deer of Rhum*. Nat. Hist. 91, 11. November 1982. (American). : series, in The Field, 14 April to 19 May 1982.

Clutton-Brock, T. H. & Ball, M. E.: *Rhum, The Natural History of an Island*. Edinburgh University Press. (A comprehensive ecological case-study).

Clutton-Brock, T., Guiness, F. E. Albon, G. D.: *Red Deer. Behaviour and ecology of two sexes*. University of Chicago Press, 1982.

Corbet, G. B. & Southern, H. N.: *The Handbook of British Mammals*. Blackwell.

Darling, F. F.: *A Herd of Red Deer*. OUP 1937. : *West Highland Survey*. OUP 1955.

Darling, F. F. &,Boyd, J. M.: *The Highlands and Islands*. Collins. (New Naturalist), (A fascinating ecological study).

Eggeling, W. J.: *Check List of the Plants of Rhum*. Trans Bot. Soc. Edinb. 1965. 40 (1) 20-59 and 40 (1) 60-99.

Emeleus, C. H. & Forster, R. M.: *Tertiary Igneous Rocks of Rhum* NNR (Field guide – stock in office).

Evans, P. R. & Flower, W. V.: *The Birds of the Small Isles*. Scottish Birds vol. 4 No. 6. 404-445. 1967.

Fitter, R., Fitter, A. & Blemey, M.: *The Wild Flowers of Britain and Northern Europe*. Collins.

Ford, D. F.: *The vegetation history of the Isle of Rhum in the Inner Hebrides*. University of Hull, Dept. of Geography 1976.

Harvie-Brown, F. A. & Buckley, T. E.: *A Vertebrate Fauna of Argyll and the Inner Hebrides*. 1892.

Heinzel, H., Fitter, R. & Parslow, J.: *The Birds of Britain and Europe*. Collins.

Holden, A. E.: *Plant Life in the Scottish Highlands*. Oliver & Boyd, 1952.

Johns, H. M.: *Collins Guide to the Ferns, Mosses and Lichens of Britain and Northern Europe*.

Johnson, S.: *A Journey to the Western Islands of Scotland 1775*, (Many reprints).

Journal Sources: Early accounts of climbing and exploring on Rhum will be found in the following: SMCJ vol. I p. 259; 3, 278; 4, 301; 10, 26; 20, 180; 24, 42. EUMCJ 1947 summer and winter numbers. F&RCCJ 1946. JMCS of Yorks, J. 1946. MAMJ 1966. Ox Mtng. 1935, 1937. York RCJ 5, 32.

Judd, J. W.: *The Tertiary Volcanoes of the Island of Rhum*. Scot. J. Geol. 1969.

Love, J. A.: *The Isle of Rum, A Short History*. (NCC office has stock – excellent booklet). : *The Return of the Sea Eagle*. Cambridge University Press. 1983. (A superbly presented book). : *The Eagles are Back*. Scots Mag. October 1985. (A popular account). : *White-Tailed Eagle Introduction on the Isle of Rhum*. Scottish Birds 11, 3. Autumn 1980.

McCann, S. B. & Richards, A.: *The Coastal Features of the Island of Rhum*. Scot J. Geol. 5 (1) 15-25, 1969.

Macculloch, J.: *A Description of the Western Isles of Scotland*. 1819.

MacEwen, L.: *A Guide to Eigg and Muck*. (Available locally and periodically revised.

Martin, M.: *A Description of the Western Islands of Scotland*. 1703 (Reprints since).

A pinnacle near the mouth of the Glen Shellesder Burn

Matthews, L. H.: *British Mammals*. Collins. (New Naturalist).

Maxwell, G.: *Harpoon at a Venture*. Hart-Davis. 1952 (& pb).

Miller, H.: *The Cruise of the Betsey*. 1858.

Mitchell, A.: *A Field Guide to the Trees of Britain and Northern Europe*. Collins.

Mitchell, B., Staines, B. W. & Welch, D.: *Ecology of Red Deer*. Inst. of Terrestrial Ecology 1977 (exhaustive bibliography).

Monro, D.: *A Description of the Western Isles of Scotland* 1549. (Reprints since).

Murray, W. H.: *The Hebrides*. Heinneman 1969. : *The Islands of Western Scotland*. Eyre Metheun 1973.

Nature Conservancy Council: *Isle of Rhum National Nature Reserve Handbook* (Thorough survey. It is periodically revised. Large bibliography). : *The Sea Eagle* (Colour booklet). : *Rhum National Nature Reserve*. (Colour booklet). : *Geology of the Isle of Rhum*. 1970. (Readable booklet). : *Tree planting* (booklet). (Most of these available from the NCC office on Rhum).

O'Dell, A. C. & Walton, K.: *The Highlands and Islands of Scotland*.

Nelson. (Physical and historical geography).

Pearsall, W. H.: *Mountains and Moorlands*. Collins (New Naturalist).

Pennent, T.: *A Tour in Scotland & Voyage to the Hebrides*. 1774.

Raven, J. & Walters, M.: *Mountain Flowers*. Collins. (New Naturalist).

Richards, M.: *The Cuillin of Rhum*. Climber and Rambler. December 1978.

Royal Commission on the Ancient & Historial Monuments of Scotland: *The Archaeological Sites and Monuments: Rhum*. (189 sites are detailed!).

Scots Magazine: *The Bulloughs of Rum*, July & Aug. 1978. (Two comprehensive, well-illustrated articles).

Scottish Mountaineering Club Journal, published each summer, gives descriptions of new routes. (Inserted in "Islands" section).

Steel, W. O. & Woodroffe, G. E.: *The Entomology of the Isle of Rhum*. Trans Soc. Brit. Ent., Vol. 18, part 6, 91-167.

Steers, J. A.: *The Sea Coast*. Collins (New Naturalist).

Steven, C.: *The Island Hills*. Hirst & Blackett. 1955.

Tennent, N.: *The Islands of Scotland* SMC General Guide. (Unreliable on Rhum route descriptions. A new Islands guide, researched by a team of authors, is due out in 1989).

Waugh, Edwin: *The Limping Pilgrim on His Wanderings*. Manchester 1883. (Pre-Bullough Rhum extensively described).

Weir, T.: *Portrait of Rum*. Scots Magazine. September 1970.

Whitehead, G. K.: *The Wild Goats of Great Britain and Ireland*. David & Charles 1972.

Wickham-Jones, C.: *Fields, Kinloch, Rhum*. (Nat. Mus. of Antiq. of Scot.).

Wickham-Jones, C. & Pollock, D.: *Revealing Rum's Past*. Scots Mag., May 1986. (Fascinating archaeological work).

Williamson, K.: *The Renaissance of Rhum*. Country Life. 3.3.77.

Williamson, K. & Boyd, J. M.: *A Mozaic of Islands*. Oliver & Boyd. 1963.

Willis, T.: *A Magical Place*. Scottish Field. December 1985.

Wormell, P.: *Establishing Woodland on the Isle of Rhum*. Scot. For. 22, 3, 207-220. : *The Manx Shearwaters of Rhum*. Scottish Birds. 9.2. Summer 1976. (edit): *The Entomology of the Isle of Rhum National Nature Reserve*. Bio. J. Li. Soc. Vol. 18 No. 4 pp291-401. December 1982.

Younge, C. M.: *The Sea Shore*. Collins (New Naturalist).

Guirdil Bothy and Bloodstone Hill

MAPS

Ordnance Survey 1:50,000 sheet 39. 1:25,000 sheets NG30/40 and NG 38/48.

Bartholomew: 1:100,000 sheet 50. Arisaig and Lochaber.

There are also vegetation and geological maps of Rhum at 1:20,000 – sometimes available from the Nature Conservancy Council.

The University of Glasgow, Dept. of Geography, have produced a 1:10,000 map to Rhum (4 sheets) 1972.

Printed by CARNMOR PRINT & DESIGN
95-97 LONDON ROAD, PRESTON, LANCASHIRE, UK.